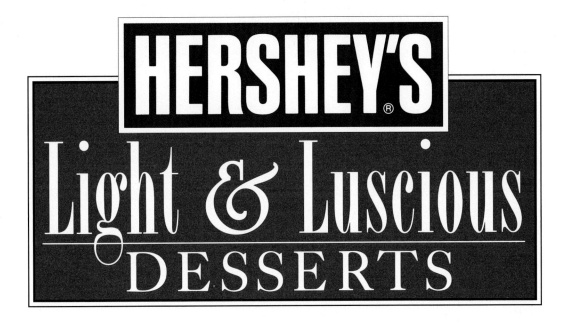

HERSHEY'S Light & Luscious DESSERTS

PUBLICATIONS INTERNATIONAL, LTD.

Copyright © 1994   **Hershey Foods Corporation.**
All rights reserved.   ®

All recipes developed and tested by The Hershey Kitchens.

This edition published by Publications International, Ltd.,
7373 N. Cicero Ave., Lincolnwood, IL 60646.

Photography: Sacco Productions Limited, Chicago.

Pictured on the front cover (*clockwise from top*): Chocolate and Raspberry Cream Torte (*page 18*), Choco-Lowfat Strawberry Shortbread Bars (*page 42*), Mini Brownie Cups (*page 44*), Chocolate Mousse Squares (*page 36*) and Chocolate Swirled Cheesecake (*page 26*).

Pictured on the back cover (*clockwise from top*): Chocolate Roulade with Creamy Yogurt Filling (*page 22*), Fruit-Filled Chocolate Dreams (*page 48*) and Tropical Chocolate Orange Ice Milk (*page 58*).

ISBN: 0-7853-0585-8

Manufactured in U.S.A.

8 7 6 5 4 3 2 1

Microwave Cooking: Microwave cooking times given in this publication are approximate. Numerous variables, such as the microwave oven's rated wattage and starting temperature, shape, amount and depth of the food, can affect cooking time. Use the cooking times as a guideline and check for doneness before adding more time. Lower wattage ovens may consistently require longer cooking times.

If you have any questions or comments about the recipes in this publication, or about any of our fine Hershey products, please write us at The Hershey Kitchens, P.O. Box 815, Hershey, PA 17033-0815, or call us, toll-free, weekdays 9 a.m. – 4 p.m. Eastern time, at 1-800-468-1714.

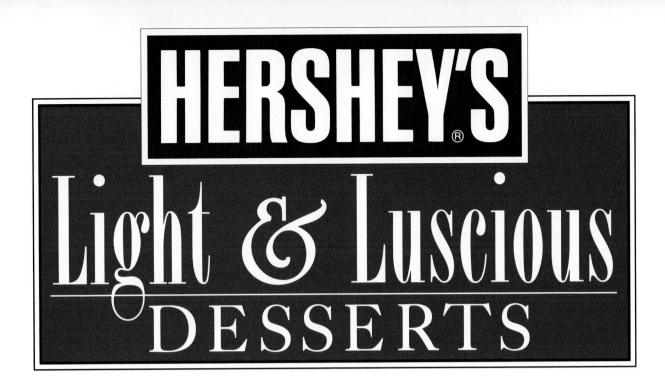

HERSHEY'S Light & Luscious DESSERTS

Introduction	4
Lightweight Cakes & Cheesecakes	6
Guilt-Free Cookies & Bars	36
Trim & Slim Desserts	48
Chocolate Potpourri	80
Index	94

Introduction

ABOUT THE RECIPES

Many Americans today are being advised to reduce the amount of fat in their diets to help keep body weight and blood cholesterol levels in check. Many others are cutting down on fat simply to look and feel better. Does this mean a final good-bye to those delectable chocolate desserts that make life sweeter? Definitely not! By using unsweetened cocoa instead of baking chocolate, chocolate lovers can experience the luscious, rich flavor they love — without all the extra fat and calories.

Hershey's Cocoa is a deep, dark chocolate baking ingredient that contains only .5 grams of fat per tablespoon and is naturally very low in sodium and cholesterol-free. Cocoa is lower in fat than other chocolate baking ingredients because most of the cocoa butter has been removed; it is the only chocolate baking ingredient listed by the American Heart Association (AHA) for use in fat-restricted diets.

The Hershey Kitchens have created a variety of luscious, flavorful desserts designed specifically for chocolate enthusiasts who want the tantalizing taste and texture of a chocolate treat without excess fat, calories and cholesterol. Each recipe has been evaluated by Hershey nutritionists for its nutritional value and has been developed using the following guidelines:

Calories — 180 or less per serving
Cholesterol — 20 mg or less per serving
Fat — 5 g or less per serving

These criteria have been established to help consumers select diets that conform with the AHA's dietary guidelines. The AHA recommends that a person's total dietary fat content be 30 percent or less of total calorie intake. Cholesterol intake should be less than 300 milligrams per day.

The analysis of each recipe includes all the ingredients that are listed in that recipe, *except* ingredients labeled as "optional." If an ingredient is presented with an option ("½ cup strawberries or raspberries") the *first* item listed was used to calculate the nutrition information. If a range is offered for an ingredient (¼ to ⅛ teaspoon, for example) the *first* amount given was used to calculate the nutrition information. Foods shown in photographs on the same serving plate and offered as "serve with" or "garnish with" suggestions at the end of a recipe are not included in the recipe analysis unless otherwise stated.

Every effort has been made to give accurate nutrition data. However, because numerous variables account for a wide range of values for certain foods, all nutrient values that appear in this publication should be considered approximate.

COCOA BASICS

Hershey's Cocoa keeps very well when stored at room temperature in the original container. It retains its freshness and quality almost indefinitely without refrigeration. Cocoa tins now feature an easy-to-use resealable plastic lid.

When storing Hershey's Cocoa, avoid contact with moisture and/or high heat; they could cause clumping and gray discoloration, although neither affect cocoa flavor or quality.

Hershey's Cocoa is a favorite ingredient in recipes developed by the Hershey Kitchens. It is so convenient to use because it is easy to measure, can be used right from the can, blends easily with other ingredients and gives desserts a rich chocolate flavor. To substitute cocoa in your favorite baked recipe, use the appropriate method listed below:

• Three level tablespoons cocoa plus 1 tablespoon shortening (liquid or solid) equals 1 square (1 ounce) unsweetened baking chocolate.

• Six level tablespoons cocoa plus 7 tablespoons sugar plus ¼ cup shortening equals one 6-ounce package (1 cup) semi-sweet chocolate chips or six squares (1 ounce each) semi-sweet chocolate.

• Three level tablespoons cocoa plus 4½ tablespoons sugar plus 2⅔ tablespoons shortening equals 1 bar (4 ounces) sweet baking chocolate.

Hershey's European Style Cocoa is also called "dutch processed" or "alkalized" cocoa. Dutching is a process that neutralizes the natural acidity found in cocoa powder. This results in a darker cocoa with a more mellow chocolate flavor than Hershey's Regular Cocoa. While European Style Cocoa imparts a different color and flavor than regular cocoa, it can easily be substituted in chocolate recipes.

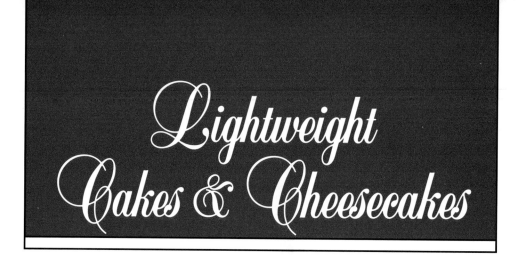

CHOCOLATE CAKE FINGERS

1 cup sugar
1 cup all-purpose flour
⅓ cup HERSHEY'S Cocoa
¾ teaspoon baking powder
¾ teaspoon baking soda
½ cup skim milk
¼ cup frozen egg substitute, thawed
¼ cup canola oil or vegetable oil

1 teaspoon vanilla extract
½ cup boiling water
   Powdered sugar
1 teaspoon freshly grated orange peel
1½ cups frozen light non-dairy whipped topping, thawed

Heat oven to 350°F. Line bottom of 13 × 9 × 2-inch baking pan with wax paper. In large mixer bowl, stir together sugar, flour, cocoa, baking powder and baking soda. Add milk, egg substitute, oil and vanilla; beat on medium speed of electric mixer 2 minutes. Stir in boiling water (batter will be thin). Pour into prepared pan.

Bake 16 to 18 minutes or until wooden pick inserted in center comes out clean. With knife or metal spatula, loosen cake from edges of pan. Place clean, lint-free dishtowel on wire rack; sprinkle lightly with powdered sugar. Invert cake on towel; peel off wax paper. Cool completely. Invert cake, right side up, on cutting board. Cut cake into small rectangles (about 2 × 1¼ inches). Stir orange peel into whipped topping; spoon dollop on each piece of cake. Garnish as desired. Store ungarnished cake, covered, at room temperature.   *42 pieces*

Nutritional Information Per Serving	
(2 pieces)	
110 Calories	0 mg Cholesterol
1 gm Protein	50 mg Sodium
15 gm Carbohydrate	15 mg Calcium
5 gm Fat	

Chocolate Cake Fingers

LUSCIOUS CHOCOLATE CHEESECAKE

2 cups (16 ounces) nonfat
    cottage cheese
¾ cup frozen egg substitute,
    thawed
⅔ cup sugar
4 ounces (½ of 8-ounce
    package) Neufchatel
    cheese (light cream
    cheese), softened

⅓ cup HERSHEY'S Cocoa or
    HERSHEY'S European
    Style Cocoa
½ teaspoon vanilla extract
    Yogurt Topping (recipe
    follows)
    Sliced strawberries or
    mandarin orange
    segments (optional)

Heat oven to 300°F. Spray 9-inch springform pan with vegetable cooking spray. In food processor, place cottage cheese, egg substitute, sugar, Neufchatel cheese, cocoa and vanilla; process until smooth. Pour into prepared pan.

Bake 35 minutes or until edge is set. Meanwhile, prepare Yogurt Topping. Carefully spread topping over top of warm cheesecake. Return cheesecake to oven; bake 5 minutes. With knife, loosen cheesecake from side of pan. Cool completely in pan on wire rack. Cover; refrigerate until chilled. Just before serving, remove side of pan. Serve with strawberries or oranges, if desired. Garnish as desired. Cover; refrigerate leftover cheesecake. *12 servings*

Yogurt Topping: In small bowl, stir together ⅔ cup plain nonfat yogurt and 2 tablespoons sugar until well blended.

Nutritional Information Per Serving

120 Calories	10 mg Cholesterol
8 gm Protein	210 mg Sodium
17 gm Carbohydrate	60 mg Calcium
3 gm Fat	

Luscious Chocolate Cheesecake

SWISS COCOA SQUARES

1 cup water
½ cup HERSHEY'S Cocoa
½ cup (1 stick) margarine
2 cups all-purpose flour
2 cups granulated sugar
½ cup frozen egg substitute,
   thawed

½ cup vanilla lowfat yogurt
1 teaspoon baking soda
½ teaspoon salt
1 tablespoon powdered
   sugar

Heat oven to 375°F. Grease and flour 15½ × 10½ × 1-inch jelly-roll pan or spray with vegetable cooking spray. In large saucepan, combine water, cocoa and margarine. Cook over medium heat, stirring frequently, until mixture comes to a boil. Remove from heat; stir in flour and granulated sugar. Add egg substitute, yogurt, baking soda and salt; mix thoroughly with spoon. Pour batter into prepared pan.

Bake 20 to 25 minutes or until wooden pick inserted in center comes out clean. Cool in pan on wire rack. Sift powdered sugar over top. Cut into squares. Store, covered, at room temperature.

32 servings

Nutritional Information Per Serving	
110 Calories	0 mg Cholesterol
2 gm Protein	105 mg Sodium
19 gm Carbohydrate	15 mg Calcium
3 gm Fat	

SLENDERIFIC BROWNIE SNACKING CAKES

½ cup all-purpose flour
½ cup HERSHEY'S Cocoa or
   HERSHEY'S European
   Style Cocoa
½ teaspoon baking powder
½ cup granulated sugar
½ cup packed light brown
   sugar

¼ cup canola oil or
   vegetable oil
½ cup egg whites (about
   4 large), beaten until
   foamy
2 teaspoons vanilla extract
   Powdered sugar (optional)

Heat oven to 350°F. Spray 8-inch square baking pan with vegetable cooking spray. In small bowl, stir together flour, cocoa and baking powder. In medium bowl, stir together granulated sugar, brown sugar and oil; stir in beaten egg whites and vanilla. Gradually stir in cocoa mixture until blended. Pour batter into prepared pan.

Bake 15 to 20 minutes or until brownie begins to pull away from sides of pan. Cool completely in pan on wire rack. Cut into bars or other desired shapes with small cookie cutters. Sift powdered sugar over tops, if desired. Store, covered, at room temperature.   *12 servings*

Nutritional Information Per Serving	
150 Calories	0 mg Cholesterol
3 gm Protein	35 mg Sodium
23 gm Carbohydrate	15 mg Calcium
5 gm Fat	

CHOCOLATE LEMON CAKE

1¼ **cups packed light brown sugar**
¾ **cup plain nonfat yogurt**
5 **egg whites**
¼ **teaspoon lemon extract**
¾ **cup all-purpose flour**
⅓ **cup HERSHEY'S Cocoa or HERSHEY'S European Style Cocoa**

¾ **teaspoon baking powder**
¾ **teaspoon baking soda**
¼ **to** ½ **teaspoon freshly grated lemon peel**
2 **teaspoons powdered sugar**
Frozen light non-dairy whipped topping, thawed (optional)

Heat oven to 350°F. Spray 9-inch square baking pan with vegetable cooking spray. In large mixer bowl, combine brown sugar, yogurt, egg whites and lemon extract; beat on medium speed of electric mixer until well blended. In small bowl, stir together flour, cocoa, baking powder and baking soda; add gradually to sugar mixture, beating until well blended. Stir in lemon peel. Pour batter into prepared pan.

Bake 35 to 40 minutes or until wooden pick inserted in center comes out clean. Cool 15 minutes; remove from pan to wire rack. Cool completely. Sift powdered sugar over top. Store, covered, at room temperature. Serve with dollops of whipped topping, if desired.

12 servings

Chocolate Orange Cake: Substitute ¼ teaspoon orange extract and ½ teaspoon freshly grated orange peel for lemon extract and lemon peel.

Nutritional Information Per Serving	
140 Calories	0 mg Cholesterol
3 gm Protein	115 mg Sodium
30 gm Carbohydrate	55 mg Calcium
0 gm Fat	

SECRET STRAWBERRY FILLED ANGEL CAKE

1 package (about
   15 ounces) angel food
   cake mix
1½ teaspoons unflavored
   gelatin
¼ cup cold water

1 container (8 ounces)
   vanilla lowfat yogurt
⅓ cup HERSHEY'S
   Strawberry Syrup
   Chocolate Syrup Whipped
   Topping (recipe follows)

Place oven rack in lowest position. Mix, bake and cool cake as directed on package. In small microwave-safe bowl, sprinkle gelatin over water; let stand 2 minutes to soften. Microwave at HIGH (100%) 40 seconds; stir thoroughly. Let stand 2 minutes or until gelatin is completely dissolved; cool slightly. In medium bowl, stir together yogurt, strawberry syrup and gelatin mixture until smooth; refrigerate until mixture mounds slightly when dropped from spoon, about 15 to 20 minutes.

Place cake, rounded side down, on cutting board. Using serrated knife, cut 1-inch layer from top of cake; lift off in one piece. Set aside. Using serrated knife, cut around cake 1 inch from center hole and 1 inch from outer edge, leaving cake walls and cake base 1¼ inches thick. Using fork, carefully remove cake in cavity without breaking through sides or bottom. Place hollowed-out cake on serving plate. Spoon strawberry syrup mixture into cavity. Cover with reserved cake top. Cover; refrigerate while preparing Chocolate Syrup Whipped Topping. Spread Chocolate Syrup Whipped Topping evenly over top and outside of cake. Refrigerate 4 hours or until strawberry syrup mixture is set before serving. Garnish as desired. Cover; refrigerate leftover cake.

18 servings

Chocolate Syrup Whipped Topping: In medium bowl, stir together 2 cups frozen light non-dairy whipped topping, thawed and ¼ cup HERSHEY'S Syrup.

Nutritional Information Per Serving

130	Calories	0 mg	Cholesterol
3 gm	Protein	100 mg	Sodium
24 gm	Carbohydrate	25 mg	Calcium
2 gm	Fat		

Secret Strawberry Filled Angel Cake

SUNBURST CHOCOLATE CAKE

5 egg whites
¾ cup sugar
½ cup all-purpose flour
⅓ cup HERSHEY'S Cocoa
½ teaspoon baking soda
¼ teaspoon salt

⅓ cup water
1 teaspoon vanilla extract
Citrus Filling (recipe follows)
Red currants (optional)

Heat oven to 375°F. Grease two 8-inch round baking pans. Line bottoms with wax paper. In small mixer bowl, beat egg whites on high speed of electric mixer 3 minutes. Gradually add sugar; continue beating 2 minutes. In small bowl, stir together flour, cocoa, baking soda and salt; add alternately with water and vanilla to sugar mixture, folding in gently until mixtures are combined. Spread batter into prepared pans.

Bake 15 to 17 minutes or until tops spring back when touched lightly in centers. Cool 5 minutes; remove from pans and peel off paper. Cool completely on wire racks. To assemble, place one cake layer on serving plate; spread half of Citrus Filling over top. Set second cake layer on top; spread remaining Citrus Filling over top. Garnish with reserved orange segments and currants, if desired. Refrigerate 2 to 3 hours or until chilled before serving. Cover; refrigerate leftover cake.

12 servings

CITRUS FILLING

1 envelope (1.3 ounces) dry whipped topping mix
½ cup cold skim milk
1 can (11 ounces) mandarin orange segments, drained and divided

¾ teaspoon grated orange peel

In small mixer bowl, beat topping mix with ½ cup milk on high speed of electric mixer until stiff peaks form. Reserve ½ cup orange segments for garnish. Cut remaining segments into thirds; gently fold into topping with orange peel.

Nutritional Information Per Serving

100 Calories	0 mg Cholesterol
3 gm Protein	110 mg Sodium
23 gm Carbohydrate	20 mg Calcium
0 gm Fat	

Sunburst Chocolate Cake

MARBLED ANGEL CAKE

1 package (about 15 ounces) angel food cake mix

¼ cup HERSHEY'S Cocoa Chocolate Glaze (recipe follows)

Place oven rack in lowest position. Heat oven to 375°F. Prepare cake batter as directed on package. Transfer 4 cups batter to medium bowl; gradually fold in cocoa until well blended, being careful not to deflate batter. Alternately pour vanilla and chocolate batters into ungreased 10-inch tube pan. With knife or metal spatula, cut through batters for marble effect.

Bake 30 to 35 minutes or until top crust is firm and looks very dry. *Do not underbake.* Invert pan on heatproof funnel or bottle; cool completely, at least 1½ hours. Carefully run knife along side of pan to loosen cake; remove from pan. Place on serving plate; drizzle with Chocolate Glaze. Let stand until set. Store, covered, at room temperature.

18 servings

Chocolate Glaze: In small saucepan, combine ⅓ cup sugar and ¼ cup water. Cook over medium heat, stirring constantly, until mixture comes to a boil. Stir until sugar dissolves; remove from heat. Immediately add 1 cup HERSHEY'S MINI CHIPS Semi-Sweet Chocolate; stir until chips are melted and mixture is smooth. Cool to desired consistency; use immediately.

Nutritional Information Per Serving	
180 Calories	0 mg Cholesterol
3 gm Protein	90 mg Sodium
33 gm Carbohydrate	5 mg Calcium
4 gm Fat	

Marbled Angel Cake

CHOCOLATE AND RASPBERRY CREAM TORTE

6 tablespoons extra light
  corn oil spread
1 cup sugar
1 cup skim milk
1 tablespoon white vinegar
½ teaspoon vanilla extract
1¼ cups all-purpose flour

⅓ cup HERSHEY'S Cocoa or
  HERSHEY'S European
  Style Cocoa
1 teaspoon baking soda
¼ cup red raspberry jam
  Raspberry Cream (recipe
  follows)

Heat oven to 350°F. Spray 15½ × 10½ × 1-inch jelly-roll pan with vegetable cooking spray. In medium saucepan over low heat, melt corn oil spread; stir in sugar. Remove from heat; stir in milk, vinegar and vanilla. In small bowl, stir together flour, cocoa and baking soda; add gradually to sugar mixture, stirring with whisk until well blended. Pour into prepared pan.

Bake 16 to 18 minutes or until wooden pick inserted in center comes out clean. Cool 10 minutes; remove from pan to wire rack. Cool completely. To assemble, cut cake crosswise into four pieces. Place one piece on serving plate; spread 1 tablespoon jam over top. Carefully spread a scant ¾ cup Raspberry Cream over jam. Repeat procedure with remaining cake layers, jam and Raspberry Cream, ending with plain layer on top. Spread remaining 1 tablespoon jam over top. Spoon or pipe remaining Raspberry Cream over jam. Refrigerate torte until ready to serve. Garnish as desired. Cover; refrigerate leftover torte.

14 servings

Raspberry Cream: Thaw and thoroughly drain 1 package (10 ounces) frozen red raspberries. In blender container, place raspberries. Cover; blend until smooth. Strain in sieve; discard seeds. In small mixer bowl, prepare 1 envelope (1.3 ounces) dry whipped topping mix as directed on package, using ½ cup cold skim milk, omitting vanilla and adding 2 to 3 drops red food color, if desired. Fold in pureed raspberries.

Nutritional Information Per Serving	
170 Calories	0 mg Cholesterol
3 gm Protein	100 mg Sodium
34 gm Carbohydrate	40 mg Calcium
3 gm Fat	

*Chocolate and Raspberry
Cream Torte*

EASY CHOCOLATE-CHEESE-FILLED ANGEL CAKE

Yogurt Cheese (recipe follows)
1 prepared angel food cake (10 inch)
⅓ cup sugar
3 tablespoons HERSHEY'S Cocoa or HERSHEY'S European Style Cocoa
2 tablespoons hot water
1½ teaspoons vanilla extract, divided
1 envelope (1.3 ounces) dry whipped topping mix
½ cup cold skim milk

Prepare Yogurt Cheese. Using serrated knife, slice cake horizontally into three layers. In medium bowl, stir together sugar, cocoa and hot water until smooth; stir in 1 teaspoon vanilla. Stir in Yogurt Cheese until well blended. Prepare topping mix as directed on package, using ½ cup milk and remaining ½ teaspoon vanilla; fold into chocolate mixture. Spread mixture between layers and on top and side of cake. Refrigerate until serving. Cover; refrigerate leftover cake.

18 servings

Yogurt Cheese: Use one 8-ounce container plain nonfat yogurt, no gelatin added. Line non-rusting colander or sieve with large piece of double thickness cheesecloth or large coffee filter; place colander over deep bowl. Spoon yogurt into prepared colander; cover with plastic wrap. Refrigerate until liquid no longer drains from yogurt, about 24 hours. Remove yogurt from cheesecloth and place in separate bowl; discard liquid.

Nutritional Information Per Serving	
120 Calories	0 mg Cholesterol
3 gm Protein	95 mg Sodium
27 gm Carbohydrate	20 mg Calcium
0 gm Fat	

COCOA CHEESECAKE WITH RICOTTA CHEESE

1³/₄ cups (15-ounce container) lowfat part-skim ricotta cheese, drained
¹/₃ cup HERSHEY'S Cocoa or HERSHEY'S European Style Cocoa
¹/₄ cup sugar
1 envelope unflavored gelatin

1 cup cold lowfat 1% milk, divided
1¹/₂ teaspoons vanilla extract, divided
1 envelope (1.3 ounces) dry whipped topping mix
Vanilla Wafer Crust (recipe follows)

In food processor or blender container, place ricotta cheese. Process until smooth. In small saucepan, stir together cocoa, sugar and gelatin; stir in ¹/₂ cup milk. Let stand 5 minutes to soften gelatin. Cook over medium heat, stirring constantly, until gelatin is completely dissolved; remove from heat. Add gelatin mixture and 1 teaspoon vanilla to ricotta cheese in food processor; blend well. Pour into medium bowl; refrigerate until mixture mounds slightly when dropped from spoon.

In cold mixer bowl, beat whipped topping mix, remaining ¹/₂ cup milk and remaining ¹/₂ teaspoon vanilla on high speed of electric mixer until stiff; fold into cocoa mixture. Pour gently over prepared Vanilla Wafer Crust. Cover; refrigerate until firm, about 4 hours. Just before serving, remove side of pan. Cover; refrigerate leftover cheesecake.

12 servings

Vanilla Wafer Crust: Heat oven to 350°F. In small bowl, stir together 10 finely crushed vanilla wafer cookies, 1 tablespoon HERSHEY'S Cocoa or HERSHEY'S European Style Cocoa and 1 tablespoon melted light corn oil spread. Press onto bottom of 8-inch springform pan. Bake 5 minutes or until set. Cool completely on wire rack.

Nutritional Information Per Serving

100 Calories	15 mg Cholesterol
6 gm Protein	75 mg Sodium
10 gm Carbohydrate	125 mg Calcium
4 gm Fat	

CHOCOLATE ROULADE WITH CREAMY YOGURT FILLING

**Creamy Yogurt Filling
(recipe on page 24)**
3 egg whites
**½ cup granulated sugar,
divided**
**1 container (8 ounces)
frozen egg substitute,
thawed**
½ cup cake flour

¼ cup HERSHEY'S Cocoa
1 teaspoon baking powder
⅛ teaspoon salt
2 tablespoons water
1 teaspoon vanilla extract
**2 teaspoons powdered sugar
Peach Sauce (recipe
on page 24)**

Prepare Creamy Yogurt Filling. Heat oven to 375°F. Line 15½×10½×1-inch jelly-roll pan with foil; spray with vegetable cooking spray. In large mixer bowl, beat egg whites on high speed of electric mixer until foamy; gradually add ¼ cup granulated sugar, beating well after each addition until stiff peaks hold their shape, sugar is dissolved and mixture is glossy. In small mixer bowl, beat egg substitute on medium speed until foamy; gradually add remaining ¼ cup granulated sugar, beating until mixture is thick. Fold egg substitute mixture into egg white mixture. In another small bowl, stir together flour, cocoa, baking powder and salt; gently fold into egg mixture alternately with water and vanilla. Spread batter evenly into prepared pan.

Bake 10 to 12 minutes or until top springs back when touched lightly in center. Immediately invert onto clean, lint-free dishtowel sprinkled with powdered sugar; peel off foil. Starting at narrow end, roll up cake and towel together. Cool completely on wire rack. Unroll cake; remove towel. Spread with Creamy Yogurt Filling to within ½ inch of edges of cake. Reroll cake; place, seam-side down, on serving plate. Cover; refrigerate 2 to 3 hours or until chilled before serving. (Cake should be eaten same day as prepared.) Serve with Peach Sauce. Garnish as desired. *10 servings*

continued on page 24

*Chocolate Roulade with Creamy
Yogurt Filling*

CREAMY YOGURT FILLING

Yogurt Cheese
(recipe follows)
1 envelope (1.3 ounces) dry
    whipped topping mix

$1/3$ cup cold skim milk
1 teaspoon vanilla extract
$1/8$ to $1/4$ teaspoon
    almond extract

Prepare Yogurt Cheese. Prepare topping mix as directed on package, using $1/3$ cup milk, 1 teaspoon vanilla and almond extract. Gently fold Yogurt Cheese into whipped topping.

Yogurt Cheese: Use one 8-ounce container plain nonfat yogurt, no gelatin added. Line non-rusting colander or sieve with large piece of double thickness cheesecloth or large coffee filter; place colander over deep bowl. Spoon yogurt into prepared colander; cover with plastic wrap. Refrigerate until liquid no longer drains from yogurt, about 24 hours. Remove yogurt from cheesecloth and place in separate bowl; discard liquid.

Peach Sauce: In blender container, place $1 1/2$ cups fresh peach slices and 1 tablespoon sugar. Cover; blend until smooth. In medium microwave-safe bowl, stir together $1/4$ cup water and $1 1/2$ teaspoons cornstarch until dissolved. Add peach mixture; stir. Microwave at HIGH (100%) $2 1/2$ to 3 minutes or until mixture boils and thickens, stirring after each minute. Cool completely.

Nutritional Information Per Serving	
140 Calories	0 mg Cholesterol
6 gm Protein	130 mg Sodium
26 gm Carbohydrate	65 mg Calcium
1 gm Fat	

CHOCOLATE CINNAMON SNACKING CAKE

$1/2$ cup evaporated skim milk
7 tablespoons light corn oil
    spread, melted
1 egg white, slightly beaten
$1/2$ teaspoon vanilla extract
$1 1/4$ cups HERSHEY'S Basic
    Cocoa Baking Mix
    (page 84)

$1/4$ teaspoon ground
    cinnamon
$1/2$ cup raisins
    Powdered Sugar Glaze
    (recipe follows)

Heat oven to 350°F. Spray 8-inch square baking pan with vegetable cooking spray. In large mixer bowl, stir together evaporated milk, corn oil spread, egg white and vanilla. Add Basic Cocoa Baking Mix and cinnamon. Beat on low speed of electric mixer until well blended. Stir in raisins. Pour batter into prepared pan.

Bake 20 to 25 minutes or until wooden pick inserted in center comes out clean. Cool completely in pan on wire rack. Drizzle with Powdered Sugar Glaze. Let stand until set. Store, covered, at room temperature. *12 servings*

Powdered Sugar Glaze: In small bowl, stir together ¼ cup powdered sugar and 1½ teaspoons warm water until of desired consistency.

Nutritional Information Per Serving

140	Calories	0 mg Cholesterol
2	gm Protein	135 mg Sodium
21	gm Carbohydrate	40 mg Calcium
5	gm Fat	

CHOCOLATE CUPCAKES

6 tablespoons light corn oil spread	1 teaspoon baking soda
1 cup sugar	Dash salt
1¼ cups all-purpose flour	1 cup lowfat buttermilk
⅓ cup HERSHEY'S Cocoa	½ teaspoon vanilla extract
	1 teaspoon powdered sugar

Heat oven to 350°F. Line 18 muffin cups (2½ inches in diameter) with paper bake cups. In large saucepan over low heat, melt corn oil spread. Remove from heat; stir in sugar. In small bowl, stir together flour, cocoa, baking soda and salt; add alternately with buttermilk and vanilla to mixture in saucepan. Stir with whisk until well blended. Fill muffin cups ⅔ full with batter.

Bake 18 to 20 minutes or until wooden pick inserted in centers comes out clean. Remove from pans to wire racks. Cool completely. Sift powdered sugar over tops of cupcakes. Store, covered, at room temperature. *18 cupcakes*

Nutritional Information Per Serving
(1 cupcake)

110	Calories	0 mg Cholesterol
2	gm Protein	85 mg Sodium
20	gm Carbohydrate	20 mg Calcium
3	gm Fat	

CHOCOLATE SWIRLED CHEESECAKE

Yogurt Cheese (recipe
follows)
2 tablespoons graham
cracker crumbs
1 package (8 ounces)
Neufchatel cheese (light
cream cheese), softened
1½ teaspoons vanilla
extract

¾ cup sugar
1 tablespoon cornstarch
1 container (8 ounces) frozen
egg substitute, thawed
¼ cup HERSHEY'S Cocoa
¼ teaspoon almond extract

Prepare Yogurt Cheese. Heat oven to 325°F. Spray bottom of 8- or 9-inch springform pan with vegetable cooking spray. Sprinkle graham cracker crumbs on bottom of pan. In large mixer bowl, beat Yogurt Cheese, Neufchatel cheese and vanilla on medium speed of electric mixer until smooth. Add sugar and cornstarch; beat just until well blended. Gradually add egg substitute, beating on low speed until blended. Transfer 1½ cups batter to medium bowl; add cocoa. Beat until well blended. Stir almond extract into vanilla batter. Alternately spoon vanilla and chocolate batters into prepared pan. With knife or metal spatula, cut through batters for marble effect.

Bake 35 minutes for 8-inch pan; 40 minutes for 9-inch pan or until edge is set. With knife, loosen cheesecake from side of pan. Cool completely in pan on wire rack. Cover; refrigerate at least 6 hours before serving. Just before serving, remove side of pan. Garnish as desired. Cover; refrigerate leftover cheesecake.   *16 servings*

Yogurt Cheese: Use one 16-ounce container plain lowfat yogurt, no gelatin added. Line non-rusting colander or sieve with large piece of double thickness cheesecloth or large coffee filter; place colander over deep bowl. Spoon yogurt into prepared colander; cover with plastic wrap. Refrigerate until liquid no longer drains from yogurt, about 24 hours. Remove yogurt from cheesecloth and place in separate bowl; discard liquid.

Nutritional Information Per Serving

100 Calories		10 mg Cholesterol
4 gm Protein		90 mg Sodium
12 gm Carbohydrate		45 mg Calcium
4 gm Fat		

Chocolate Swirled Cheesecake

HERSHEY'S SLIMMED DOWN CHOCOLATE CAKE

1¼ cups all-purpose flour
⅓ cup HERSHEY'S Cocoa
1 teaspoon baking soda
6 tablespoons extra light corn oil spread
1 cup sugar
1 cup skim milk

1 tablespoon white vinegar
½ teaspoon vanilla extract
Slimmed Down Cocoa Frosting or Slimmed Down Cocoa Almond Frosting (recipes follow)

Heat oven to 350°F. Spray two 8-inch round baking pans with vegetable cooking spray. In small bowl, stir together flour, cocoa and baking soda. In medium saucepan over low heat, melt corn oil spread; stir in sugar. Remove from heat. Add milk, vinegar and vanilla to mixture in saucepan; stir. Add flour mixture; stir with whisk until well blended. Pour batter into prepared pans.

Bake 20 minutes or until wooden pick inserted in centers comes out clean. Cool 10 minutes; remove from pans to wire racks. Cool completely. To assemble, place one cake layer on serving plate; spread half of frosting over top. Set second cake layer on top; spread remaining frosting over top. Refrigerate 2 to 3 hours or until chilled before serving. Garnish as desired. Cover; refrigerate leftover cake.

12 servings

Slimmed Down Cocoa Frosting: In small mixer bowl, stir together 1 envelope (1.3 ounces) dry whipped topping mix, ½ cup cold skim milk, 1 tablespoon HERSHEY'S Cocoa and ½ teaspoon vanilla extract. Beat on high speed of electric mixer until soft peaks form.

Slimmed Down Cocoa Almond Frosting: Prepare Slimmed Down Cocoa Frosting, substituting ¼ teaspoon almond extract for the ½ teaspoon vanilla extract.

Nutritional Information Per Serving	
160 Calories	0 mg Cholesterol
3 gm Protein	115 mg Sodium
28 gm Carbohydrate	45 mg Calcium
4 gm Fat	

Hershey's Slimmed Down Chocolate Cake

CHOCOLATE CHERRY ANGEL DELIGHT

⅓ cup HERSHEY'S Cocoa
1 package (about
    15 ounces) "two-step"
    angel food cake mix
1 envelope (1.3 ounces) dry
    whipped topping mix

½ cup cold skim milk
½ teaspoon vanilla extract
1 can (20 ounces) reduced-
    calorie cherry pie filling,
    chilled

Place oven rack in lowest position. In small bowl, sift cocoa over contents of cake flour packet; stir to blend. Proceed with mixing cake as directed on package. Bake and cool as directed for 10-inch tube pan. Carefully run knife along side of pan to loosen cake; remove from pan. Using serrated knife, slice cake horizontally into three layers. Prepare topping mix as directed on package, using ½ cup milk and ½ teaspoon vanilla. Fold half of pie filling into whipped topping. Place bottom cake layer on serving plate; spread half of whipped topping mixture over top. Set second cake layer on top; spread remaining whipped topping mixture over top. Set third cake layer on top; spread remaining cherry pie filling over top. Serve Immediately. Cover; refrigerate leftover cake.   *14 servings*

Nutritional Information Per Serving

170 Calories	0 mg Cholesterol
4 gm Protein	135 mg Sodium
39 gm Carbohydrate	15 mg Calcium
0 gm Fat	

FOUR WAY FUDGEY CHOCOLATE CAKE

1¼ cups all-purpose flour
1 cup sugar
1 cup skim milk
⅓ cup HERSHEY'S Cocoa or
    HERSHEY'S European
    Style Cocoa
⅓ cup unsweetened
    applesauce
1 tablespoon white vinegar
1 teaspoon baking soda

½ teaspoon vanilla extract
Toppings (optional):
    Frozen light non-dairy
    whipped topping,
    thawed, REESE'S Peanut
    Butter Chips, sliced
    strawberries, chopped
    almonds, powdered
    sugar

Heat oven to 350°F. Spray 9-inch square baking pan with vegetable cooking spray. In large mixer bowl, stir together all ingredients except Toppings; beat on low speed of electric mixer until blended. Pour batter into prepared pan.

Bake 30 to 35 minutes or until wooden pick inserted in center comes out clean. Cool completely in pan on wire rack. For optional toppings, if desired, spoon whipped topping into pastry bag fitted with small star tip; pipe stars in two lines to divide cake into four squares. Pipe stars into one square; press one peanut butter chip into each star. Place strawberries into another square. Sprinkle almonds into third square. Lightly sift powdered sugar over remaining square. Serve immediately. Cover; refrigerate leftover cake. Store ungarnished cake, covered, at room temperature.

12 servings

Nutritional Information Per Serving

130	Calories	0	mg Cholesterol
3	gm Protein	80	mg Sodium
29	gm Carbohydrate	30	mg Calcium
0	gm Fat		

COCOA APPLE SNACK CAKE

1 cup chopped Golden
   Delicious apple
   (1 medium)
²⁄₃ cup sugar
⅛ teaspoon ground
   cinnamon
1½ cups all-purpose flour
¼ cup HERSHEY'S Cocoa

1 teaspoon baking soda
¼ teaspoon salt
1 cup water
¼ cup canola oil or
   vegetable oil
1 teaspoon lemon juice
1 teaspoon vanilla extract
½ teaspoon powdered sugar

Heat oven to 350°F. Spray 8- or 9-inch square baking pan with vegetable cooking spray. In small bowl, stir together apple, sugar and cinnamon. In large bowl, stir together flour, cocoa, baking soda and salt. In another small bowl, combine water, oil, lemon juice and vanilla; add to flour mixture, beating with whisk or fork just until batter is smooth. Fold in apple mixture. Pour batter into prepared pan.

Bake 30 to 35 minutes or until wooden pick inserted in center comes out clean. Cool slightly in pan on wire rack. Sift powdered sugar over top. Serve warm or cool. Store, covered, at room temperature.

12 servings

Nutritional Information Per Serving

150	Calories	0	mg Cholesterol
2	gm Protein	115	mg Sodium
24	gm Carbohydrate	5	mg Calcium
5	gm Fat		

FUDGEY CHOCOLATE CUPCAKES

³/₄ **cup water**
½ **cup (1 stick) light corn oil**
  spread, melted
2 **egg whites, slightly beaten**
1 **teaspoon vanilla extract**
2¼ **cups HERSHEY'S Basic**
  Cocoa Baking Mix
  (page 84)

2 **teaspoons powdered sugar**
2 **teaspoons HERSHEY'S**
  Cocoa (optional)

Heat oven to 350°F. Line 16 muffin cups (2½ inches in diameter) with foil or paper bake cups. In large mixer bowl, stir together water, corn oil spread, egg whites and vanilla. Add Basic Cocoa Baking Mix; beat on low speed of electric mixer until blended. Fill muffin cups ⅔ full with batter.

Bake 20 to 25 minutes or until wooden pick inserted in centers comes out clean. Remove from pans to wire racks. Cool completely. Sift powdered sugar over tops of cupcakes. If desired, partially cover part of each cupcake with paper cutout. Sift cocoa over exposed powdered sugar. Carefully lift off cutout. Store, covered, at room temperature.   *16 cupcakes*

Nutritional Information Per Serving (1 cupcake)			
110	Calories	0	mg Cholesterol
2	gm Protein	150	mg Sodium
17	gm Carbohydrate	10	mg Calcium
4	gm Fat		

Fudgey Chocolate Cupcakes

ELEGANT CHOCOLATE ANGEL TORTE

⅓ cup HERSHEY'S Cocoa
1 package (about 15 ounces) "two-step" angel food cake mix
2 envelopes (1.3 ounces each) dry whipped topping mix

1 cup cold skim milk
1 teaspoon vanilla extract
1 cup strawberry puree*
16 strawberries

Place oven rack in lowest position. In small bowl, sift cocoa over contents of cake flour packet; stir to blend. Proceed with mixing cake as directed on package. Bake and cool as directed for 10-inch tube pan. Carefully run knife along side of pan to loosen cake; remove from pan. Using serrated knife, slice cake horizontally into four layers. Prepare topping mixes as directed on packages, using 1 cup milk and 1 teaspoon vanilla. Blend in strawberry puree.

To assemble, place bottom cake layer on serving plate; spread one-fourth of topping over top. Set next cake layer on top; spread with one-fourth of topping. Repeat procedure with remaining cake layers and topping, ending with topping. Garnish with strawberries. Refrigerate until ready to serve. Slice cake with sharp serrated knife; cut with gentle sawing motion. Cover; refrigerate leftover cake.

16 servings

Mash 2 cups sliced fresh strawberries (or frozen berries, thawed) or place in blender container or food processor. Cover; blend until smooth. Puree should measure 1 cup.

Nutritional Information Per Serving	
100 Calories	0 mg Cholesterol
3 gm Protein	80 mg Sodium
22 gm Carbohydrate	50 mg Calcium
0 gm Fat	

TRIMMED DOWN CHOCOBERRY CHEESECAKE

- 1 cup (8 ounces) nonfat cottage cheese
- 1 package (8 ounces) Neufchatel cheese (light cream cheese), softened
- 1 cup sugar
- 1/3 cup HERSHEY'S Cocoa or HERSHEY'S European Style Cocoa
- 1 package (10 ounces) frozen strawberries in syrup, thawed and drained
- 1/3 cup frozen egg substitute, thawed
- Graham Crust (recipe follows)
- Frozen light non-dairy whipped topping, thawed (optional)
- Additional strawberries (optional)

Heat oven to 325°F. In food processor, place cottage cheese; process until smooth. Add Neufchatel cheese, sugar, cocoa and 1 package strawberries; process until smooth. Stir in egg substitute. Pour gently over prepared Graham Crust.

Bake 55 to 60 minutes or just until almost set in center. With knife, loosen cheesecake from side of pan. Cool completely in pan on wire rack. Cover; refrigerate until chilled. Just before serving, remove side of pan. Serve with whipped topping and additional strawberries, if desired. Cover; refrigerate leftover cheesecake.   *14 servings*

Graham Crust: In small bowl, stir together 1/2 cup graham cracker crumbs and 1 tablespoon melted margarine; press onto bottom of 8-inch springform pan.

Nutritional Information Per Serving

160	Calories	15	mg Cholesterol
5	gm Protein	150	mg Sodium
23	gm Carbohydrate	25	mg Calcium
5	gm Fat		

CHOCOLATE MOUSSE SQUARES

¾ **cup plus 2 tablespoons**
all-purpose flour, divided
⅔ **cup plus 3 tablespoons**
granulated sugar, divided
¼ **cup (½ stick) margarine**
¼ **cup HERSHEY'S Cocoa**
½ **teaspoon powdered instant**
coffee

¼ **teaspoon baking powder**
½ **cup frozen egg substitute,**
thawed
½ **teaspoon vanilla extract**
½ **cup plain lowfat yogurt**
½ **teaspoon powdered sugar**

Heat oven to 350°F. In medium bowl, stir together ¾ cup flour and
3 tablespoons granulated sugar. With pastry blender or 2 knives,
cut in margarine until fine crumbs form. Press mixture onto bottom of
ungreased 8-inch square baking pan. Bake 15 minutes or until golden.
Reduce oven temperature to 300°F.

Meanwhile, in small mixer bowl, stir together remaining ⅔ cup
granulated sugar, cocoa, remaining 2 tablespoons flour, instant
coffee and baking powder. Add egg substitute and vanilla; beat on
medium speed of electric mixer until well blended. Add yogurt; beat
just until blended. Pour over prepared crust.

Bake 30 minutes or until center is set. Cool completely in pan on wire
rack. Cut into squares. If desired, place small paper cutouts over top.
Sift powdered sugar over cutouts. Carefully remove cutouts. Store,
covered, in refrigerator.   *16 squares*

Nutritional Information Per Serving	
(1 square)	
100 Calories	0 mg Cholesterol
2 gm Protein	55 mg Sodium
16 gm Carbohydrate	20 mg Calcium
3 gm Fat	

Chocolate Mousse Squares

DOUBLE CHOCOLATE SUGAR COOKIES

2 egg whites, slightly beaten
¼ cup light corn oil spread, melted
1 tablespoon water
1 teaspoon vanilla extract

2½ cups HERSHEY'S Basic Cocoa Baking Mix (see page 84)
¼ cup sugar
Chocolate Glaze (recipe follows)

Heat oven to 350°F. Lightly spray cookie sheet with vegetable cooking spray. In medium bowl, stir together egg whites, corn oil spread, water and vanilla. Stir in Basic Cocoa Baking Mix until well blended. Shape dough into 1-inch balls. Roll in sugar to coat. Place 2 inches apart on prepared cookie sheet. Press balls flat with bottom of glass.

Bake 6 to 8 minutes or until set. Cool 5 minutes; remove from cookie sheet to wire rack. Cool completely. Drizzle Chocolate Glaze over tops of cookies. Let stand until set. Store, covered, at room temperature.   *2½ dozen cookies*

Chocolate Glaze: In small microwave-safe bowl, place ¼ cup HERSHEY'S Semi-Sweet Chocolate Chips and ½ teaspoon shortening (do not use butter, margarine or oil). Microwave at HIGH (100%) 30 seconds; stir. If necessary, microwave at HIGH an additional 30 seconds or until chips are melted and mixture is smooth when stirred. Use immediately.

Nutritional Information Per Serving	
(1 cookie with glaze)	
70 Calories	0 mg Cholesterol
1 gm Protein	75 mg Sodium
13 gm Carbohydrate	5 mg Calcium
2 gm Fat	

CHOCOLATE ORANGE MERINGUES

3 egg whites
½ teaspoon vanilla extract
⅛ teaspoon orange extract
¾ cup sugar

¼ cup HERSHEY'S Cocoa
½ teaspoon freshly grated orange peel

Heat oven to 300°F. Cover cookie sheet with parchment paper or foil. In large mixer bowl, beat egg whites, vanilla and orange extract on high speed of electric mixer until soft peaks form. Gradually add sugar, beating well after each addition until stiff peaks hold their shape, sugar is dissolved and mixture is glossy. Sprinkle half of cocoa and all of orange peel over egg white mixture; gently fold in just until combined. Repeat with remaining cocoa. Spoon mixture into pastry bag fitted with large star tip; pipe 1½-inch diameter stars onto prepared cookie sheet.

Bake 35 to 40 minutes or until dry. Cool slightly; peel paper from cookies. Cool completely on wire rack. Store, covered, at room temperature. *5 dozen cookies*

Nutritional Information Per Serving
(1 cookie)

12	Calories	0	mg Cholesterol
0	gm Protein	5	mg Sodium
3	gm Carbohydrate	0	mg Calcium
0	gm Fat		

FUDGEY BROWNIE CUT-OUTS

1 cup granulated sugar
⅔ cup all-purpose flour
½ cup HERSHEY'S Cocoa
½ cup applesauce
2 egg whites

1 teaspoon vanilla extract
¼ cup finely chopped nuts
½ teaspoon powdered sugar

Heat oven to 350°F. Line 8-inch square baking pan with foil, extending foil over sides of pan; spray with vegetable cooking spray. In small mixer bowl, stir together granulated sugar, flour and cocoa. Add applesauce, egg whites and vanilla; beat on medium speed of electric mixer until well blended. Stir in nuts. Spread batter into prepared pan.

Bake 25 minutes or until edges are firm. Cool completely in pan on wire rack. Place in freezer about 15 minutes for easier cutting. Lift brownies from pan using sides of foil; carefully peel off foil. Cut into squares or other desired shapes with small cookie cutters. Sift powdered sugar over tops of brownies. Store, covered, at room temperature. *16 brownies*

Nutritional Information Per Serving
(1 brownie)

90	Calories	0	mg Cholesterol
2	gm Protein	10	mg Sodium
18	gm Carbohydrate	5	mg Calcium
2	gm Fat		

SUNNY COCOA DROP COOKIES

½ cup (1 stick) light corn oil spread
⅔ cup granulated sugar
⅔ cup lowfat sour cream
1 egg white
1 teaspoon vanilla extract
¼ teaspoon freshly grated orange peel
1¾ cups all-purpose flour

3 tablespoons HERSHEY'S Cocoa
1 teaspoon baking soda
½ teaspoon baking powder
¼ teaspoon ground cinnamon
Cocoa Glaze (recipe follows)

Heat oven to 350°F. Spray cookie sheet with vegetable cooking spray. In large mixer bowl, beat corn oil spread and sugar on medium speed of electric mixer until light and fluffy. Add sour cream, egg white, vanilla and orange peel; beat until well blended. In small bowl, stir together flour, cocoa, baking soda, baking powder and cinnamon; add gradually to sugar mixture, beating until blended. Drop dough by rounded teaspoonfuls onto prepared cookie sheet.

Bake 10 to 12 minutes or until set. Remove from cookie sheet to wire rack. Cool completely. Drizzle Cocoa Glaze over tops of cookies. Let stand until set. Store, covered, at room temperature.

4 dozen cookies

COCOA GLAZE

1 tablespoon light corn oil spread
2 tablespoons water
1 tablespoon HERSHEY'S Cocoa

½ cup powdered sugar
½ teaspoon vanilla extract

In small saucepan over low heat, melt corn oil spread. Stir in water and cocoa. Cook, stirring constantly, until thick. *Do not boil.* Remove from heat; gradually add powdered sugar and vanilla, beating with spoon or whisk to drizzling consistency.

Nutritional Information Per Serving	
(2 cookies with glaze)	
100 Calories	0 mg Cholesterol
1 gm Protein	50 mg Sodium
14 gm Carbohydrate	5 mg Calcium
4 gm Fat	

Sunny Cocoa Drop Cookies

CHOCO-LOWFAT STRAWBERRY SHORTBREAD BARS

¼ **cup (½ stick) light corn oil spread**
½ **cup sugar**
1 **egg white**
1¼ **cups all-purpose flour**
¼ **cup HERSHEY'S Cocoa or HERSHEY'S European Style Cocoa**
¾ **teaspoon cream of tartar**

½ **teaspoon baking soda**
Dash salt
½ **cup strawberry all-fruit spread**
Vanilla Chip Drizzle (recipe follows)

Heat oven to 375°F. Lightly spray 13×9×2-inch baking pan with vegetable cooking spray. In mixer bowl, combine corn oil spread and sugar; beat on medium speed of electric mixer until well blended. Add egg white; beat until well blended. In small bowl, stir together flour, cocoa, cream of tartar, baking soda and salt; beat gradually into sugar mixture. Gently press mixture onto bottom of prepared pan.

Bake 10 to 12 minutes or just until set. Cool completely in pan on wire rack. Spread fruit spread evenly over crust. Cut into bars or other desired shapes with small cookie cutters. Drizzle Vanilla Chip Drizzle over tops of bars. Let stand until set. Store, covered, at room temperature. *3 dozen bars*

Vanilla Chip Drizzle: In small microwave-safe bowl, place ⅓ cup HERSHEY'S Vanilla Milk Chips and ½ teaspoon shortening (do not use butter, margarine or oil). Microwave at HIGH (100%) 30 seconds; stir vigorously. If necessary, microwave at HIGH an additional 15 seconds until chips are melted and mixture is smooth when stirred. Use immediately.

Nutritional Information Per Serving
(1 bar with drizzle)

50 Calories	0 mg Cholesterol
1 gm Protein	45 mg Sodium
10 gm Carbohydrate	5 mg Calcium
1 gm Fat	

Choco-Lowfat Strawberry Shortbread Bars

MINI BROWNIE CUPS

¼ cup (½ stick) light corn oil
  spread
2 egg whites
1 egg
¾ cup sugar
⅔ cup all-purpose flour

⅓ cup HERSHEY'S Cocoa
½ teaspoon baking powder
¼ teaspoon salt
  Mocha Glaze (recipe
  follows)

Heat oven to 350°F. Line 24 small muffin cups (1¾ inches in diameter) with paper bake cups or spray with vegetable cooking spray. In small saucepan over low heat, melt corn oil spread; cool slightly. In small mixer bowl, beat egg whites and egg on medium speed of electric mixer until foamy; gradually add sugar, beating until slightly thickened and light in color. In small bowl, stir together flour, cocoa, baking powder and salt; add gradually to egg mixture, beating until blended. Gradually add corn oil spread; beat just until blended. Fill muffin cups ⅔ full with batter.

Bake 15 to 18 minutes or until wooden pick inserted in centers comes out clean. Remove from pans to wire racks. Cool completely. Drizzle Mocha Glaze over tops of brownie cups. Let stand until set. Store, covered, at room temperature.   *2 dozen brownie cups*

MOCHA GLAZE

¼ cup powdered sugar
¾ teaspoon HERSHEY'S
  Cocoa
¼ teaspoon powdered
  instant coffee

2 teaspoons hot water
¼ teaspoon vanilla extract

In small bowl, stir together powdered sugar and cocoa. Dissolve coffee in water; add to sugar mixture, stirring until well blended. Stir in vanilla.

Nutritional Information Per Serving	
(1 brownie cup with glaze)	
60 Calories	10 mg Cholesterol
1 gm Protein	50 mg Sodium
10 gm Carbohydrate	5 mg Calcium
2 gm Fat	

Mini Brownie Cups

CHOCOLATE MINT MERINGUES

3 egg whites
¾ teaspoon vanilla extract
¾ cup sugar

¼ cup HERSHEY'S Cocoa
Chocolate Mint Glaze
(recipe follows)

Heat oven to 300°F. Cover cookie sheet with parchment paper. In large mixer bowl, beat egg whites and vanilla on high speed of electric mixer until foamy. Beat in sugar, 1 tablespoon at a time, beating well after each addition until stiff peaks hold their shape, sugar is dissolved and mixture is glossy. Sift about half of cocoa over egg white mixture; gently fold in just until combined. Repeat with remaining cocoa. Spoon mixture into pastry bag fitted with large star tip; pipe 2-inch diameter stars onto prepared cookie sheet.

Bake 35 to 45 minutes or until dry. Cool slightly; peel paper from cookies. Cool completely on wire rack. Line tray or cookie sheet with wax paper. Dip half of each cookie into Chocolate Mint Glaze; place on prepared tray until set (refrigerate, if desired). Store, covered, in refrigerator.   *3 dozen cookies*

Chocolate Mint Glaze: In small microwave-safe bowl, place ½ cup HERSHEY'S Semi-Sweet Chocolate Chips and 2 teaspoons shortening (do not use butter, margarine or oil). Microwave at HIGH (100%) 1 minute or until chips are melted and mixture is smooth when stirred. Stir in 2 to 3 drops mint extract. Use immediately.

Nutritional Information Per Serving
(1 cookie with glaze)

35	Calories	0 mg Cholesterol
1 gm	Protein	5 mg Sodium
6 gm	Carbohydrate	0 mg Calcium
1 gm	Fat	

CHOCOLATE CLOUDS

3 egg whites
⅛ teaspoon cream of tartar
¾ cup sugar
1 teaspoon vanilla extract
2 tablespoons HERSHEY'S
Cocoa

1¾ cups (10-ounce package)
HERSHEY'S Semi-Sweet
Chocolate Chunks *or*
2 cups (12-ounce
package) HERSHEY'S
Semi-Sweet Chocolate
Chips

Heat oven to 300°F. Cover cookie sheet with parchment paper or foil. In large mixer bowl, beat egg whites and cream of tartar on high speed of electric mixer until soft peaks form. Gradually add sugar and vanilla, beating well after each addition until stiff peaks hold their shape, sugar is dissolved and mixture is glossy. Sift cocoa over egg white mixture; gently fold in just until combined. Fold in chocolate chunks. Drop mixture by heaping tablespoonfuls onto prepared cookie sheet.

Bake 35 to 45 minutes or just until dry. Cool slightly; peel paper from cookies. Cool completely on wire rack. Store, covered, at room temperature.   *2½ dozen cookies*

Nutritional Information Per Serving
(1 cookie)

80 Calories	0 mg Cholesterol
1 gm Protein	15 mg Sodium
12 gm Carbohydrate	5 mg Calcium
3 gm Fat	

CRISPY COCOA BARS

¼ **cup (½ stick) margarine**
¼ **cup HERSHEY'S Cocoa**

5 cups (10½-ounce package) miniature marshmallows
5 cups crisp rice cereal

Grease 13×9×2-inch pan. In large saucepan over low heat, melt margarine; stir in cocoa and marshmallows. Cook over low heat, stirring constantly, until marshmallows are melted and mixture is smooth and well blended. Continue cooking and stirring 1 minute. Remove from heat. Add cereal; stir until well coated. With lightly greased spatula or wax paper, press mixture evenly into prepared pan. Cool completely. Cut into bars. Store, covered, at room temperature.   *2 dozen bars*

Nutritional Information Per Serving
(1 bar)

80 Calories	5 mg Cholesterol
1 gm Protein	95 mg Sodium
16 gm Carbohydrate	5 mg Calcium
2 gm Fat	

FRUIT-FILLED CHOCOLATE DREAMS

1 envelope (1.3 ounces) dry
    whipped topping mix
1 tablespoon HERSHEY'S
    Cocoa
½ cup cold skim milk

½ teaspoon vanilla extract
Assorted fresh fruit,
    cut up
Chocolate Sauce (recipe
    follows)

Place foil on cookie sheet. In small mixer bowl, stir together topping mix and cocoa. Add ½ cup milk and ½ teaspoon vanilla. Beat on high speed of electric mixer until stiff peaks form. Spoon topping into 5 mounds onto prepared cookie sheet. With spoon, shape into 4-inch shells. Freeze until firm, about 1 hour. To serve, fill center of each frozen shell with about ⅓ cup assorted fresh fruit; drizzle with 1 tablespoon Chocolate Sauce. Garnish as desired. Serve immediately.

5 servings

CHOCOLATE SAUCE

¾ cup sugar
⅓ cup HERSHEY'S Cocoa
1 tablespoon cornstarch

¾ cup water
1 tablespoon margarine
1 teaspoon vanilla extract

In small saucepan, combine sugar, cocoa and cornstarch; gradually stir in water. Cook over medium heat, stirring constantly, until mixture comes to a boil; boil 1 minute. Remove from heat; add margarine and vanilla, stirring until smooth. Cover; refrigerate until cold.

Nutritional Information Per Serving

130 Calories	0 mg Cholesterol
2 gm Protein	25 mg Sodium
27 gm Carbohydrate	45 mg Calcium
1 gm Fat	

Fruit-Filled Chocolate Dreams

LUSCIOUS COLD CHOCOLATE SOUFFLES

1 envelope unflavored gelatin
¼ cup cold water
2 tablespoons reduced-calorie tub margarine
1½ cups cold skim milk, divided
½ cup sugar
⅓ cup HERSHEY'S Cocoa or HERSHEY'S European Style Cocoa
2½ teaspoons vanilla extract, divided
1 envelope (1.3 ounces) dry whipped topping mix

Measure lengths of foil to fit around 6 small souffle dishes (about 4 ounces each); fold in thirds lengthwise. Tape securely to outside of dishes to form collar, allowing collar to extend 1 inch above rims of dishes. Lightly oil inside of foil.

In small microwave-safe bowl, sprinkle gelatin over water; let stand 2 minutes to soften. Microwave at HIGH (100%) 40 seconds; stir thoroughly. Stir in margarine until melted; let stand 2 minutes or until gelatin is completely dissolved. In small mixer bowl, stir together 1 cup milk, sugar, cocoa and 2 teaspoons vanilla. Beat on low speed of electric mixer while gradually pouring in gelatin mixture. Beat until well blended. Prepare topping mix as directed on package, using remaining ½ cup milk and remaining ½ teaspoon vanilla; carefully fold into chocolate mixture until well blended.

Spoon into prepared souffle dishes, filling ½-inch from top of collars. Cover; refrigerate until firm, about 3 hours. Carefully remove foil. Garnish as desired.

6 servings

Note: Six (6-ounce) custard cups may be used in place of souffle dishes; omit foil collar.

Nutritional Information Per Serving	
150 Calories	0 mg Cholesterol
4 gm Protein	55 mg Sodium
27 gm Carbohydrate	80 mg Calcium
3 gm Fat	

Luscious Cold Chocolate Souffles

CARIBBEAN FREEZE

²/₃ cup sugar
3 tablespoons HERSHEY'S
    Cocoa
1³/₄ cups water

3 tablespoons frozen
    pineapple juice
    concentrate, thawed
1 tablespoon golden rum *or*
½ teaspoon rum extract

In medium saucepan, stir together sugar and cocoa; stir in water. Cook over medium heat, stirring occasionally, until mixture comes to a boil. Reduce heat; simmer 3 minutes, stirring occasionally. Cool completely. Stir concentrate and rum into chocolate mixture. Cover; refrigerate until cold, about 6 hours. Pour into 1-quart ice cream freezer container. Freeze according to manufacturer's directions. Garnish as desired.

6 servings

Nutritional Information Per Serving	
150 Calories	0 mg Cholesterol
1 gm Protein	5 mg Sodium
36 gm Carbohydrate	10 mg Calcium
0 gm Fat	

COCOA PUDDING

¼ cup sugar
3 tablespoons HERSHEY'S
    Cocoa
3 tablespoons cornstarch
2 cups lowfat 1% milk
1 teaspoon vanilla extract

Frozen light non-dairy
    whipped topping,
    thawed (optional)
Fresh strawberries
    (optional)

In medium saucepan, stir together sugar, cocoa and cornstarch; gradually stir in milk. Cook over medium heat, stirring constantly, until mixture comes to a boil; boil and stir 1 minute. Remove from heat; stir in vanilla. Pour into 4 individual dessert dishes. Press plastic wrap directly onto surface. Cool; refrigerate until cold. Top with whipped topping and strawberries, if desired.

4 servings

Nutritional Information Per Serving	
140 Calories	5 mg Cholesterol
5 gm Protein	65 mg Sodium
26 gm Carbohydrate	155 mg Calcium
2 gm Fat	

Caribbean Freeze

TIDAL WAVE COCOA ALMOND MOUSSE

²/₃ cup sugar
¹/₃ cup HERSHEY'S Cocoa
1 envelope unflavored
 gelatin
1¹/₂ cups (12-ounce can)
 evaporated skim milk

¹/₂ teaspoon almond extract
1 envelope (1.3 ounces) dry
 whipped topping mix
¹/₂ cup cold skim milk
¹/₂ teaspoon vanilla extract

In medium saucepan, stir together sugar, cocoa and gelatin; stir in evaporated milk until blended. Let stand 1 minute to soften gelatin. Cook over low heat, stirring constantly, until gelatin is completely dissolved, about 5 minutes. Remove from heat; pour mixture into large bowl. Stir in almond extract. Refrigerate, stirring occasionally, until mixture mounds slightly when dropped from spoon.

Prepare topping mix as directed on package, using ½ cup milk and ½ teaspoon vanilla. Reserve ½ cup topping for garnish (cover and refrigerate until ready to use); fold remaining topping into chocolate mixture. Let stand a few minutes; spoon into 7 individual dessert dishes. Cover; refrigerate until firm. Garnish with reserved topping.

7 servings

Nutritional Information Per Serving	
160 Calories	0 mg Cholesterol
6 gm Protein	70 mg Sodium
31 gm Carbohydrate	170 mg Calcium
1 gm Fat	

CHOCOLATE-BANANA YOGURT FREEZE

³/₄ cup sugar
¹/₄ cup HERSHEY'S Cocoa
1¹/₂ cups (12-ounce can)
 evaporated skim milk

1 container (8 ounces) plain
 nonfat yogurt
¹/₃ cup ripe mashed banana
1 teaspoon vanilla extract

In medium microwave-safe bowl or 4-cup measure, stir together sugar and cocoa. Stir in evaporated milk. Microwave at HIGH (100%) 2 to 3 minutes or until mixture comes to a boil; stir with whisk until smooth. Refrigerate 30 minutes. Stir in yogurt, banana and vanilla. Cover; refrigerate until cold, about 6 hours.

Pour mixture into 1-quart ice cream freezer container. Freeze according to manufacturer's directions. (If harder texture is desired, spoon into freezerproof container; cover and place in freezer until of desired consistency.)

8 servings

Nutritional Information Per Serving

140 Calories	0 mg Cholesterol
6 gm Protein	80 mg Sodium
29 gm Carbohydrate	200 mg Calcium
0 gm Fat	

CHOCOLATE-ORANGE ICE

2 cups water
⅔ cup sugar
2 tablespoons HERSHEY'S Cocoa

Strips of peel from 1 orange
½ cup fresh orange juice

In medium saucepan, stir together water, sugar, cocoa and orange peel. Cook over medium heat, stirring constantly, until mixture comes to a boil. Reduce heat; simmer 5 minutes, without stirring. Strain to remove orange peel; discard. Cover; refrigerate mixture several hours until cold.

Stir orange juice into chocolate mixture. Pour into 1-quart ice cream freezer container. Freeze according to manufacturer's directions.

6 servings

Nutritional Information Per Serving

100 Calories	0 mg Cholesterol
1 gm Protein	5 mg Sodium
24 gm Carbohydrate	10 mg Calcium
0 gm Fat	

FRUIT IN A CHOCOLATE CLOUD

Yogurt Cheese (recipe
  follows)
2 cups (1 pint) fresh
  strawberries, rinsed and
  drained
1/4 cup sugar
1/4 cup HERSHEY'S Cocoa or
  HERSHEY'S European
  Style Cocoa
2 tablespoons hot water

2 teaspoons vanilla extract,
  divided
1/2 to 1 teaspoon freshly
  grated orange peel
  (optional)
2 envelopes (1.3 ounces
  each) dry whipped
  topping mix
1 cup cold skim milk
2 large bananas, sliced

Prepare Yogurt Cheese. Remove hulls of strawberries; cut strawberries in half vertically. In medium bowl, stir together sugar, cocoa and water until smooth and well blended. Stir in 1 teaspoon vanilla. Gradually stir in Yogurt Cheese and orange peel, if desired; blend thoroughly. In large mixer bowl, prepare topping mixes as directed on packages, using 1 cup milk and remaining 1 teaspoon vanilla; fold into chocolate mixture.

Into 1 1/2-quart glass serving bowl, carefully spoon half of chocolate mixture; place one-half of strawberry halves, cut sides out, around inside of entire bowl. Layer banana slices over chocolate mixture. Cut remaining strawberry halves into smaller pieces; layer over banana slices. Carefully spread remaining chocolate mixture over fruit. Cover; refrigerate several hours before serving. Garnish as desired.

12 servings

Yogurt Cheese: Use two 8-ounce containers vanilla lowfat yogurt, no gelatin added. Line non-rusting colander or sieve with large piece of double thickness cheesecloth or large coffee filter; place colander over deep bowl. Spoon yogurt into prepared colander; cover with plastic wrap. Refrigerate until liquid no longer drains from yogurt, about 24 hours. Remove yogurt from cheesecloth and place in separate bowl; discard liquid.

Nutritional Information Per Serving	
110 Calories	5 mg Cholesterol
3 gm Protein	35 mg Sodium
20 gm Carbohydrate	75 mg Calcium
1 gm Fat	

Fruit in a Chocolate Cloud

TROPICAL CHOCOLATE ORANGE ICE MILK

⅔ **cup nonfat dry milk powder**
⅔ **cup sugar**
¼ **cup HERSHEY'S Cocoa**
2 **tablespoons cornstarch**
4 **cups (1 quart) skim milk, divided**
¼ **teaspoon freshly grated orange peel**

⅛ **teaspoon orange extract**
Orange Cups (optional, directions follow)
Additional freshly grated orange peel (optional)

In medium saucepan, stir together milk powder, sugar, cocoa and cornstarch. Gradually stir in 2 cups skim milk. Cook over medium heat, stirring constantly, until mixture is smooth and slightly thickened, about 5 minutes. Remove from heat. Stir in remaining 2 cups milk, ¼ teaspoon orange peel and orange extract. Cover; refrigerate several hours until cold.

Pour mixture into 2-quart ice cream freezer container. Freeze according to manufacturer's directions. Before serving, let stand at room temperature until slightly softened. Scoop ½ cup ice milk into each Orange Cup or 8 individual dessert dishes. Garnish with additional orange peel, if desired. *8 servings*

Orange Cups: Cut about 1-inch slice from tops of 8 oranges; discard. Using sharp knife, cut out and remove small triangle shaped notches around tops of oranges to make zig-zag pattern. Scoop out pulp; reserve for other uses.

Nutritional Information Per Serving	
150 Calories	5 mg Cholesterol
7 gm Protein	95 mg Sodium
28 gm Carbohydrate	225 mg Calcium
1 gm Fat	

Tropical Chocolate Orange Ice Milk

CHOCOLATE-FILLED MERINGUE SHELLS WITH STRAWBERRY SAUCE

2 egg whites
¼ teaspoon cream of tartar
   Dash salt
¾ cup sugar
¼ teaspoon vanilla extract

Chocolate Filling (recipe follows)
1 package (10 ounces) frozen strawberries in syrup, thawed

Heat oven to 275°F. Line 10 muffin cups (2½ inches in diameter) with paper bake cups. In small mixer bowl, beat egg whites with cream of tartar and salt at high speed of electric mixer until soft peaks form. Beat in sugar, 1 tablespoon at a time, beating well after each addition until stiff peaks hold their shape, sugar is dissolved and mixture is glossy. Fold in vanilla. Spoon about 3 tablespoons mixture in each muffin cup. Using back of spoon or small spatula, push mixture up sides of muffin cups forming well in center.

Bake 1 hour or until meringues turn delicate cream color and feel dry to the touch. Cool in pan on wire rack. Before serving, carefully remove paper from shells. For each serving, spoon 1 heaping tablespoonful Chocolate Filling into meringue shell. In blender container, place strawberries with syrup. Cover; blend until smooth. Spoon over filled shells. Garnish as desired. To store leftover unfilled shells, peel paper bake cups from remaining shells; store shells loosely covered at room temperature.   *10 servings*

Chocolate Filling: In small mixer bowl, beat 4 ounces (½ of 8-ounce package) softened Neufchatel cheese (light cream cheese) and ¼ cup HERSHEY'S Cocoa on medium speed of electric mixer until blended. Gradually add ¾ cup powdered sugar, beating until well blended. Fold in 1 cup frozen light non-dairy whipped topping, thawed.

Nutritional Information Per Serving	
170 Calories	10 mg Cholesterol
3 gm Protein	95 mg Sodium
32 gm Carbohydrate	10 mg Calcium
4 gm Fat	

Chocolate-Filled Meringue Shells with Strawberry Sauce

COCOA-BANANA FREEZE

¼ **cup sugar**
¼ **cup HERSHEY'S Cocoa**
1½ **cups (12-ounce can)
evaporated skim milk**
¼ **cup light corn syrup**

1 **container (8 ounces) plain
nonfat yogurt**
1 **ripe medium banana,
mashed**

In medium saucepan, stir together sugar and cocoa; stir in evaporated milk. Cook over medium heat, stirring constantly, until sugar is dissolved. Remove from heat; stir in corn syrup. Cool completely.

Add yogurt and banana to chocolate mixture; stir with whisk until well blended. Cover; refrigerate several hours until cold. Pour mixture into 1-quart ice cream freezer container. Freeze according to manufacturer's directions. *8 servings*

Nutritional Information Per Serving	
130 Calories	5 mg Cholesterol
6 gm Protein	85 mg Sodium
25 gm Carbohydrate	205 mg Calcium
1 gm Fat	

SILKY COCOA CREME

1 **envelope unflavored gelatin**
¼ **cup cold water**
½ **cup sugar**
⅓ **cup HERSHEY'S Cocoa**
¾ **cup skim milk**
½ **cup lowfat part-skim
ricotta cheese**

1 **teaspoon vanilla extract**
½ **cup frozen light non-dairy
whipped topping, thawed**
Fresh strawberries (optional)

In small bowl, sprinkle gelatin over water; let stand 2 minutes to soften. In medium saucepan, stir together sugar and cocoa; stir in milk. Cook over medium heat, stirring constantly, until mixture is very hot. Add gelatin mixture, stirring until gelatin is completely dissolved; pour mixture into medium bowl. Refrigerate until mixture is slightly cold (do not allow to gel).

In blender container or food processor, blend ricotta cheese and vanilla until smooth; stir into whipped topping. Gradually fold into chocolate mixture; immediately pour into 2-cup mold. Cover; refrigerate until firm, about 2 to 3 hours. Unmold onto serving plate. Serve with strawberries, if desired. *8 servings*

Note: Eight individual dessert dishes may be used in place of 2-cup mold, if desired.

Nutritional Information Per Serving

110 Calories	5 mg Cholesterol
4 gm Protein	35 mg Sodium
17 gm Carbohydrate	75 mg Calcium
3 gm Fat	

CHOCOLATE DESSERT TIMBALES

1 envelope unflavored gelatin
½ cup cold water
⅓ cup sugar
3 tablespoons HERSHEY'S Cocoa
1½ cups lowfat milk
2 egg yolks, slightly beaten
2 teaspoons vanilla extract

1 cup frozen light non-dairy whipped topping, thawed
Additional frozen light non-dairy whipped topping, thawed (optional)
Fresh or canned fruit slices, drained (optional)

In small bowl, sprinkle gelatin over water; let stand 5 minutes to soften. In medium saucepan, combine sugar and cocoa; stir in milk. Stir in egg yolks. Cook over medium heat, stirring constantly, until mixture just begins to boil; remove from heat. Add gelatin mixture and vanilla; stir until gelatin is completely dissolved. Pour mixture into medium bowl. Refrigerate, stirring occasionally, until mixture starts to thicken, about 1 hour.

Carefully fold 1 cup whipped topping into chocolate mixture, blending until smooth. Pour into 7 small custard cups. Cover; refrigerate until firm. Unmold onto 7 dessert dishes, if desired. Garnish with additional whipped topping and fruit slices, if desired. *7 servings*

Nutritional Information Per Serving

110 Calories	65 mg Cholesterol
4 gm Protein	30 mg Sodium
13 gm Carbohydrate	75 mg Calcium
5 gm Fat	

CREAMY CHOCOLATE AND PEACH LAYERED PUDDING

⅓ **cup sugar**
¼ **cup HERSHEY'S Cocoa**
3 **tablespoons cornstarch**
2⅔ **cups lowfat 2% milk**
1 **teaspoon vanilla extract**

Peach Sauce (recipe follows)
⅓ **cup frozen light non-dairy whipped topping, thawed**

In medium saucepan, stir together sugar, cocoa and cornstarch; gradually stir in milk. Cook over medium heat, stirring constantly, until mixture comes to a boil; boil 1 minute. Remove from heat; stir in vanilla. Press plastic wrap directly onto surface. Cool completely.

Meanwhile, prepare Peach Sauce. In 6 individual dessert dishes, layer chocolate mixture and Peach Sauce. Cover; refrigerate until cold. Serve with dollop of whipped topping. Garnish as desired.

6 servings

Peach Sauce: In blender container, place 1½ cups fresh peach slices and 1 tablespoon sugar. Cover; blend until smooth. In medium microwave-safe bowl, stir together ¼ cup water and 1½ teaspoons cornstarch until smooth. Add peach mixture; stir. Microwave at HIGH (100%) 2½ to 3 minutes or until mixture boils, stirring after each minute. Cool completely.

Nutritional Information Per Serving	
180 Calories	10 mg Cholesterol
5 gm Protein	55 mg Sodium
29 gm Carbohydrate	145 mg Calcium
5 gm Fat	

Creamy Chocolate and Peach Layered Pudding

FROSTY CHOCOLATE AND VANILLA MINI BOMBES

6 tablespoons extra-light
   corn oil spread
1 cup sugar
1 cup skim milk
1 tablespoon white vinegar
½ teaspoon vanilla extract
1¼ cups all-purpose flour
⅓ cup HERSHEY'S Cocoa or
   HERSHEY'S European
   Style Cocoa

1 teaspoon baking soda
1 cup vanilla nonfat frozen
   yogurt, slightly softened
Light Cocoa Frosting
   (recipe follows)

Heat oven to 350°F. Line 16 muffin cups (2½ inches in diameter) with paper bake cups. In medium saucepan over low heat, melt corn oil spread; stir in sugar. Remove from heat; stir in milk, vinegar and vanilla. In small bowl, stir together flour, cocoa and baking soda; add gradually to sugar mixture, stirring with whisk until well blended. Fill muffin cups ½ full with batter.

Bake 16 to 18 minutes or until wooden pick inserted in centers comes out clean. Remove from pans to wire racks. Cool completely. Place foil on cookie sheet. Remove paper from cupcakes. Cut about 1-inch cone-shaped piece from top center of each cupcake; remove. Cut tips from cones, leaving ¼-inch thick base; discard tips. Reserve bases. Fill each cupcake with 1 tablespoon frozen yogurt. Place reserved base onto yogurt portion; press. Place filled cakes, cut side down, on prepared cookie sheet; freeze at least 45 minutes.

Spread 2 tablespoons Light Cocoa Frosting on top and sides of each cupcake. Freeze until frosting is firm, about 2 hours. Let stand at room temperature 15 minutes before serving. Garnish as desired. Cover; freeze leftover bombes. *16 servings*

Light Cocoa Frosting: In small mixer bowl, stir together 1 envelope (1.3 ounces) dry whipped topping mix, ½ cup cold skim milk, 1 tablespoon HERSHEY'S Cocoa and ½ teaspoon vanilla extract. Beat on high speed of electric mixer until soft peaks form.

Nutritional Information Per Serving	
140 Calories	0 mg Cholesterol
3 gm Protein	95 mg Sodium
27 gm Carbohydrate	50 mg Calcium
3 gm Fat	

Frosty Chocolate and Vanilla
Mini Bombes

SHAMROCK PARFAITS

1 **envelope unflavored gelatin**
½ **cup cold water**
¾ **cup sugar**
½ **cup HERSHEY'S Cocoa**
1¼ **cups evaporated skim milk**
1 **teaspoon vanilla extract**

2 **cups frozen light non-dairy whipped topping, thawed, divided**
⅛ **teaspoon mint extract**
6 **to 7 drops green food color**

In medium saucepan, sprinkle gelatin over water; let stand 2 minutes to soften. Cook over low heat, stirring constantly, until gelatin is completely dissolved, about 3 minutes. In small bowl, stir together sugar and cocoa; add gradually to gelatin mixture, stirring with whisk until well blended. Continue to cook over low heat, stirring constantly, until sugar is dissolved, about 3 minutes. Remove from heat. Stir in evaporated milk and vanilla. Pour mixture into large bowl. Refrigerate, stirring occasionally, until mixture mounds slightly when dropped from spoon, about 20 minutes.

Fold ½ cup whipped topping into chocolate mixture. Divide about half of mixture evenly among 8 parfait or wine glasses. Stir extract and food color into remaining 1½ cups topping; divide evenly among glasses. Spoon remaining chocolate mixture over topping in each glass. Garnish as desired. Serve immediately or cover and refrigerate until serving time.

8 servings

Nutritional Information Per Serving	
160 Calories	0 mg Cholesterol
5 gm Protein	50 mg Sodium
25 gm Carbohydrate	125 mg Calcium
5 gm Fat	

Shamrock Parfaits

LIGHTER THAN AIR CHOCOLATE DELIGHT

2 envelopes unflavored
   gelatin
1/2 cup cold water
1 cup boiling water
1 1/3 cups nonfat dry milk
   powder
1/3 cup HERSHEY'S Cocoa or
   HERSHEY'S European
   Style Cocoa

1 tablespoon vanilla extract
Dash salt
Granulated sugar
   substitute to equal
   14 teaspoons sugar
8 large ice cubes

In blender container, sprinkle gelatin over cold water; let stand 4 minutes to soften. Gently stir with rubber spatula, scraping gelatin particles off sides; add boiling water to gelatin mixture. Cover; blend until gelatin dissolves. Add milk powder, cocoa, vanilla and salt; blend on medium speed until well mixed. Add sugar substitute and ice cubes; blend on high speed until ice is crushed and mixture is smooth and fluffy. Immediately pour into 4-cup mold. Cover; refrigerate until firm. Unmold onto serving plate. *8 servings*

Note: Eight individual dessert dishes may be used in place of 4-cup mold, if desired.

Nutritional Information Per Serving

70 Calories	0 mg Cholesterol
6 gm Protein	105 mg Sodium
9 gm Carbohydrate	145 mg Calcium
1 gm Fat	

CHOCO-ORANGE FLUFF

1/3 cup sugar
1/4 cup HERSHEY'S Cocoa
1 envelope unflavored
   gelatin
2 cups skim milk
1 teaspoon vanilla extract
1/8 to 1/4 teaspoon orange
   extract
1 1/2 cups frozen light non-dairy
   whipped topping,
   thawed

Additional frozen light
   non-dairy whipped
   topping, thawed
   (optional)
Fresh orange wedges
   (optional)

In medium saucepan, stir together sugar, cocoa and gelatin. Stir in milk; let stand 2 minutes to soften gelatin. Cook over medium heat, stirring constantly, until gelatin is completely dissolved, about 5 minutes. Pour mixture into medium bowl; stir in vanilla and orange extract. Refrigerate, stirring occasionally, until mixture mounds slightly when dropped from spoon (do not allow to gel).

Add 1½ cups whipped topping to chocolate mixture; beat with whisk until well blended. Refrigerate about 10 minutes to thicken slightly. Spoon into 8 individual dessert dishes. Cover; refrigerate until firm, 3 to 4 hours. Garnish with additional whipped topping and orange wedges, if desired. *8 servings*

Nutritional Information Per Serving

110	Calories	0	mg Cholesterol
4	gm Protein	35	mg Sodium
14	gm Carbohydrate	85	mg Calcium
4	gm Fat		

SLIMMING CHOCOLATE MOUSSE

1 teaspoon unflavored gelatin	1 envelope (1.3 ounces) dry
1 tablespoon cold water	whipped topping mix
2 tablespoons boiling water	½ cup cold lowfat 2% milk
¼ cup sugar	1 teaspoon vanilla extract
¼ cup HERSHEY'S Cocoa	

In small cup, sprinkle gelatin over cold water; let stand 1 minute to soften. Add boiling water; stir until gelatin is completely dissolved. In small bowl, stir together sugar and cocoa. Add gelatin mixture; stir until well blended. Prepare topping mix as directed on package, using ½ cup milk and 1 teaspoon vanilla. Beat on high speed of electric mixer until stiff peaks form. Gradually add chocolate mixture; continue beating on high speed until well blended. Spoon into 4 individual dessert dishes. Cover; refrigerate until firm, about 2 hours. *4 servings*

Nutritional Information Per Serving

140	Calories	0	mg Cholesterol
3	gm Protein	20	mg Sodium
24	gm Carbohydrate	45	mg Calcium
1	gm Fat		

CHOCOLATE-BANANA SHERBET

2 ripe medium bananas
1 cup apricot nectar *or*
    peach or pineapple
    juice, divided

½ cup **HERSHEY'S Semi-Sweet**
    Chocolate Chips
2 tablespoons sugar
1 cup lowfat 2% milk

Into blender container or food processor, slice bananas. Add ¾ cup fruit juice. Cover; blend until smooth. In small microwave-safe bowl, place chocolate chips, remaining ¼ cup fruit juice and sugar. Microwave at HIGH (100%) 30 seconds; stir. If necessary, microwave at HIGH an additional 15 seconds at a time, stirring after each heating, just until chips are melted and mixture is smooth when stirred. Add to mixture in blender. Cover; blend until thoroughly combined. Add milk. Cover; blend until smooth. Pour into 8- or 9-inch square pan. Cover; freeze until hard around edges, about 2 hours.

In large mixer bowl or food processor, spoon partially frozen mixture; beat until smooth but not melted. Return mixture to pan. Cover; freeze until firm, stirring several times before mixture freezes. Before serving, let stand at room temperature 10 to 15 minutes until slightly softened. Scoop into 8 individual dessert dishes.

8 servings

Nutritional Information Per Serving	
130 Calories	5 mg Cholesterol
2 gm Protein	15 mg Sodium
22 gm Carbohydrate	45 mg Calcium
4 gm Fat	

Chocolate-Banana Sherbet

WAIST-WATCHER'S COCOA DESSERT

1 envelope unflavored
   gelatin
1³/₄ cups cold water
²/₃ cup nonfat dry milk powder
2 egg yolks, slightly beaten
3 tablespoons HERSHEY'S
   Cocoa
¹/₄ teaspoon salt
¹/₂ cup sugar or equivalent
   amount of granulated
   sugar substitute

2 teaspoons vanilla extract
¹/₂ cup frozen light non-dairy
   whipped topping, thawed
Assorted fresh fruit, cut up
   (optional)
Additional frozen light
   non-dairy whipped
   topping, thawed
   (optional)
Additional HERSHEY'S
   Cocoa (optional)

In medium saucepan, sprinkle gelatin over water; let stand 5 minutes to soften. Add milk powder, egg yolks, 3 tablespoons cocoa and salt. Cook over medium heat, stirring constantly, until mixture begins to boil; remove from heat. Stir in sugar and vanilla. Pour mixture into large bowl. Refrigerate, stirring occasionally, until mixture mounds slightly when dropped from spoon, about 1 hour.

Fold ½ cup whipped topping into chocolate mixture. Pour into 6 individual dessert dishes. Cover; refrigerate until firm, about 4 hours. Garnish individual dessert dishes with assorted fresh fruit or additional whipped topping, sprinkled with additional cocoa, if desired.

6 servings

Note: A 3-cup mold may be used in place of individual dessert dishes, if desired.

Nutritional Information Per Serving		
140 Calories	70 mg Cholesterol	
5 gm Protein	135 mg Sodium	
23 gm Carbohydrate	105 mg Calcium	
3 gm Fat		

Waist-Watcher's Cocoa Dessert

REFRESHING COCOA-FRUIT SHERBET

1 ripe medium banana
1½ cups orange juice
1 cup (½ pint) half-and-half

½ cup sugar
¼ cup HERSHEY'S Cocoa

Into blender container, slice banana. Add orange juice; cover and blend until smooth. Add remaining ingredients; cover and blend well. Pour into 8- or 9-inch square pan. Cover; freeze until hard around edges.

Into blender container or large mixer bowl, spoon partially frozen mixture. Cover; blend until smooth but not melted. Pour into 1-quart mold. Cover; freeze until firm. Unmold onto cold plate and slice. Garnish as desired.   *8 servings*

Variation: Add 2 teaspoons orange-flavored liqueur with orange juice.

Nutritional Information Per Serving

140	Calories	10	mg Cholesterol
3	gm Protein	15	mg Sodium
24	gm Carbohydrate	45	mg Calcium
4	gm Fat		

CHOCOLATE YOGURT CREME PUDDING

1 cup sugar
⅓ cup HERSHEY'S Cocoa
1 envelope unflavored
  gelatin
1⅓ cups lowfat 2% milk

2 cups vanilla lowfat yogurt
1 teaspoon vanilla extract
  Fresh raspberries or sliced
  strawberries (optional)

In medium saucepan, stir together sugar, cocoa and gelatin; stir in milk. Let stand 5 minutes to soften gelatin. Cook over medium heat, stirring constantly, until mixture comes to a boil and gelatin is completely dissolved. Cool slightly. Add yogurt and vanilla; fold in just until blended. Pour into 8 individual dessert dishes. Cover; refrigerate until firm, about 6 hours. Serve with fruit, if desired.   *8 servings*

Nutritional Information Per Serving

180	Calories	5	mg Cholesterol
6	gm Protein	25	mg Sodium
32	gm Carbohydrate	150	mg Calcium
2	gm Fat		

Refreshing Cocoa-Fruit Sherbet

LIGHTER THAN AIR
CHOCOLATE ALMOND PARFAITS

1 cup sugar, divided
⅓ cup plus 1 tablespoon water, divided
1 container (8 ounces) frozen egg substitute, thawed
3 tablespoons all-purpose flour
¼ cup HERSHEY'S Cocoa or HERSHEY'S European Style Cocoa

2 tablespoons reduced-calorie margarine
½ teaspoon almond extract
2 envelopes (1.3 ounces each) dry whipped topping mix
1 cup cold skim milk
1 teaspoon vanilla extract

In small saucepan, stir together ⅔ cup sugar and ⅓ cup water; cook over medium heat, stirring constantly, until sugar is dissolved and mixture comes to a boil. Boil, without stirring, 5 minutes; remove from heat. Meanwhile, in large mixer bowl, beat egg substitute at medium speed of electric mixer until frothy. Gradually add flour, 1 tablespoon at a time, beating thoroughly. Gradually beat hot sugar mixture into egg mixture; continue beating until cool, about 5 minutes.

In small microwave-safe bowl, stir together remaining ⅓ cup sugar, cocoa, margarine and remaining 1 tablespoon water. Microwave at HIGH (100%) 1 to 1½ minutes or until mixture is smooth when stirred. Cool slightly. Pour 1 cup egg mixture into another small bowl; stir in almond extract, blending well. Blend chocolate mixture into remaining egg mixture. Prepare topping mixes as directed on packages, using 1 cup milk and 1 teaspoon vanilla. Fold 1½ cups whipped topping into egg mixture. Fold remaining whipped topping into chocolate mixture.

Divide about half of egg mixture evenly among 11 parfait or wine glasses; top with half of chocolate mixture. Repeat layering with remaining mixtures. Cover; freeze until firm, about 8 hours. Before serving, let stand at room temperature 5 minutes. *11 servings*

Nutritional Information Per Serving

170	Calories	0 mg	Cholesterol
4 gm	Protein	65 mg	Sodium
28 gm	Carbohydrate	45 mg	Calcium
4 gm	Fat		

TEMPTING CHOCOLATE MOUSSE

1 envelope unflavored gelatin
2½ cups skim milk
¼ cup HERSHEY'S Cocoa or
   HERSHEY'S European Style
   Cocoa
1 tablespoon cornstarch
1 egg yolk

1 teaspoon vanilla extract
  Granulated sugar substitute
   to equal 8 teaspoons
   sugar
1 cup prepared sucrose-free
  whipped topping*

In medium saucepan, sprinkle gelatin over milk; let stand 5 minutes to soften. Stir in cocoa, cornstarch and egg yolk; cook over medium heat, stirring constantly with whisk, until mixture comes to a boil. Reduce heat to low; cook, stirring constantly, until mixture thickens slightly, about 1 minute. Remove from heat; cool to lukewarm. Stir in vanilla and sugar substitute. Pour mixture into medium bowl. Refrigerate, stirring occasionally, until thickened, about 45 minutes.

Fold 1 cup prepared whipped topping into chocolate mixture. Spoon into 6 individual dessert dishes. Cover; refrigerate until firm. Garnish with remaining whipped topping, if desired. *6 servings*

Prepare 1 envelope (1 ounce) sucrose-free dry whipped topping mix with ½ cup very cold water according to package directions. (This makes about 2 cups topping; use 1 cup topping for mousse. Reserve remainder for garnishing, if desired.)

Nutritional Information Per Serving	
90 Calories	35 mg Cholesterol
9 gm Protein	55 mg Sodium
11 gm Carbohydrate	135 mg Calcium
3 gm Fat	

ORANGE CHOCOLATE CHIP BREAD

½ cup skim milk
½ cup plain nonfat yogurt
⅓ cup sugar
¼ cup orange juice
1 egg, slightly beaten
1 tablespoon freshly grated
   orange peel

3 cups all-purpose biscuit
   baking mix
½ cup HERSHEY'S MINI CHIPS
   Semi-Sweet Chocolate

Heat oven to 350°F. Grease 9×5×3-inch loaf pan or spray with vegetable cooking spray. In large bowl, stir together milk, yogurt, sugar, orange juice, egg and orange peel; add baking mix. With spoon, beat until well blended, about 1 minute. Stir in small chocolate chips. Pour into prepared pan.

Bake 45 to 50 minutes or until wooden pick inserted in center comes out clean. Cool 10 minutes; remove from pan to wire rack. Cool completely before slicing. Garnish as desired. Wrap leftover bread in foil or plastic wrap. Store at room temperature or freeze for longer storage.

1 loaf (16 slices)

Nutritional Information Per Serving	
(1 slice)	
150 Calories	15 mg Cholesterol
3 gm Protein	280 mg Sodium
23 gm Carbohydrate	30 mg Calcium
5 gm Fat	

Orange Chocolate Chip Bread

CHOCOLATE CREAM PIE WITH SKIM MILK

⅓ **cup sugar**
¼ **cup cornstarch**
3 **tablespoons HERSHEY'S Cocoa or HERSHEY'S European Style Cocoa**
2 **cups skim milk**
1 **teaspoon vanilla extract**

1 **packaged graham cracker crumb crust (6 ounces)**
Frozen light non-dairy whipped topping, thawed (optional)
Assorted fresh fruit (optional)

To Microwave: In large microwave-safe bowl, stir together sugar, cornstarch and cocoa; gradually stir in milk. Microwave at HIGH (100%) 2 minutes; stir well. Microwave at HIGH 2 to 5 minutes or until mixture just begins to boil; stir well. Microwave at HIGH 30 seconds to 1 minute or until mixture is very hot and thickened. Stir in vanilla. Pour into crust. Press plastic wrap directly onto surface; refrigerate several hours or until set. Garnish with whipped topping and fruit, if desired. Store, covered, in refrigerator.

10 servings

Nutritional Information Per Serving

160 Calories	0 mg Cholesterol
3 gm Protein	145 mg Sodium
25 gm Carbohydrate	65 mg Calcium
5 gm Fat	

COCOA FRUIT BALLS

2½ **cups (about 12 ounces) mixed dried fruits, such as apples, apricots, pears and prunes**
1¼ **cups (8 ounces) dried Mission figs**

1 **cup flaked coconut**
½ **cup HERSHEY'S Cocoa**
2 **tablespoons orange juice**
2 **tablespoons honey**
¼ **cup powdered sugar**

Remove pits from prunes and stems from figs, if necessary. Using metal blade of food processor, process dried fruits, figs and coconut until ground and almost paste-like (or put through fine blade of food grinder). In large bowl, combine cocoa, orange juice and honey with fruit mixture; mix well. Cover; refrigerate until chilled. Shape mixture into 1¼-inch balls. Store in airtight container at room temperature for 3 to 4 days. Store in airtight container in refrigerator or freezer for longer storage. Roll in powdered sugar just before serving.

3 dozen balls

Nutritional Information Per Serving
(1 ball rolled in powdered sugar)

70 Calories	0 mg Cholesterol
1 gm Protein	10 mg Sodium
14 gm Carbohydrate	15 mg Calcium
1 gm Fat	

PEANUT BUTTER 'N' CHOCOLATE CHIPS SNACK MIX

6 cups bite-size crisp corn, rice or wheat squares cereal
3 cups miniature pretzels
2 cups toasted oat cereal rings

1 cup raisins or dried fruit bits
1 cup HERSHEY'S Semi-Sweet Chocolate Chips
1 cup REESE'S Peanut Butter Chips

In large bowl, stir together all ingredients. Store in airtight container at room temperature.

14 cups snack mix

Nutritional Information Per Serving
(½ cup)

120 Calories	0 mg Cholesterol
3 gm Protein	105 mg Sodium
19 gm Carbohydrate	15 mg Calcium
4 gm Fat	

SLIMMING CHOCOBERRY SPLASH

Crushed ice
¾ cup cold skim milk
¼ cup sliced fresh
   strawberries
2 tablespoons HERSHEY'S
   Syrup

2 tablespoons vanilla
   ice milk
2 tablespoons club soda

Fill tall glass with crushed ice. In blender container, place all remaining ingredients except club soda. Cover; blend until smooth. Pour into glass over crushed ice; add club soda. Serve immediately. Garnish as desired.

Two 6-ounce servings

Variations:
Substitute any of the following for strawberries:
   ⅓ cup drained canned peach slices
   3 tablespoons frozen raspberries
   2 pineapple slices *or* ¼ cup drained crushed canned pineapple

Nutritional Information Per Serving
100 Calories	5 mg Cholesterol
4 gm Protein	70 mg Sodium
18 gm Carbohydrate	140 mg Calcium
1 gm Fat	

HERSHEY'S BASIC COCOA BAKING MIX

4½ cups all-purpose flour
2¾ cups sugar
1¼ cups HERSHEY'S Cocoa
1 tablespoon plus
   ½ teaspoon baking
   powder

1¾ teaspoons salt
1¼ teaspoons baking soda

In large bowl, stir together all ingredients. Store in airtight container in cool, dry place for up to 1 month. Stir before using.

8 cups mix

Note: Nutritional information is not given for this recipe. This mix is used to prepare other baked goods, see pages 24, 32 and 38.

Slimming Chocoberry Splash

SINFULLY RICH NONFAT FUDGE SAUCE

½ cup sugar
¼ cup HERSHEY'S Cocoa or
    HERSHEY'S European
    Style Cocoa
1 tablespoon plus
    1 teaspoon cornstarch
½ cup evaporated skim milk

2 teaspoons vanilla extract
Assorted fresh fruit,
    cut up (optional)
Cake (optional)
Nonfat frozen yogurt
    (optional)

In small saucepan, stir together sugar, cocoa and cornstarch; gradually stir in evaporated milk. Cook over low heat, stirring constantly with whisk, until mixture boils; continue cooking and stirring until thickened and smooth. Remove from heat; stir in vanilla. Serve warm or cold with assorted fresh fruit, cake or nonfat frozen yogurt, if desired. Cover; refrigerate leftover sauce. *7 servings*

Nutritional Information Per Serving
(2 tablespoons sauce)

80 Calories	0 mg Cholesterol
2 gm Protein	25 mg Sodium
19 gm Carbohydrate	55 mg Calcium
0 gm Fat	

PEACHY CHOCOLATE YOGURT SHAKE

⅔ cup peeled fresh peach
    slices *or* 1 package
    (10 ounces) frozen peach
    slices, thawed and
    drained

¼ teaspoon almond extract
2 cups (1 pint) vanilla nonfat
    frozen yogurt
¼ cup HERSHEY'S Syrup
¼ cup skim milk

In blender container, place peaches and almond extract. Cover; blend until smooth. Add frozen yogurt, syrup and milk. Cover; blend until smooth. Serve immediately. *Four 6-ounce servings*

Nutritional Information Per Serving

150 Calories	0 mg Cholesterol
4 gm Protein	85 mg Sodium
34 gm Carbohydrate	20 mg Calcium
0 gm Fat	

Sinfully Rich Nonfat Fudge Sauce

SKIM MILK HOT COCOA

3 tablespoons sugar
2 tablespoons HERSHEY'S
   Cocoa

¼ cup hot water
1½ cups skim milk
⅛ teaspoon vanilla extract

In small saucepan, stir together sugar and cocoa; gradually stir in water. Cook over medium heat, stirring constantly, until mixture boils; boil and stir 2 minutes. Immediately stir in milk; continue cooking and stirring until mixture is hot. *Do not boil.* Remove from heat; stir in vanilla. Serve immediately. *Two 7-ounce servings*

Nutritional Information Per Serving

160 Calories	5 mg Cholesterol
8 gm Protein	100 mg Sodium
29 gm Carbohydrate	235 mg Calcium
1 gm Fat	

CHOCOLATE SAUCE AND ICE MILK

2 tablespoons margarine
⅓ cup sugar
2 tablespoons HERSHEY'S
   Cocoa
2 tablespoons light corn
   syrup

¼ cup evaporated skim milk
1 teaspoon vanilla extract
   Vanilla ice milk

In small saucepan over low heat, melt margarine. Remove from heat; stir in sugar, cocoa and corn syrup. Stir in evaporated milk. Cook over low heat, stirring constantly, just until mixture begins to boil and is smooth. Remove from heat; stir in vanilla. Cool slightly. Spoon 1 tablespoon warm sauce over ½ cup vanilla ice milk for each serving. Cover; refrigerate leftover sauce. *12 servings*

Nutritional Information Per Serving
(1 tablespoon sauce with ½ cup ice milk)

150 Calories	10 mg Cholesterol
3 gm Protein	85 mg Sodium
24 gm Carbohydrate	105 mg Calcium
5 gm Fat	

CHOCOLATE FRUIT DIP

1 container (8 ounces)
   vanilla lowfat yogurt
¹/₃ cup packed light brown
   sugar
1 tablespoon HERSHEY'S
   Cocoa

½ teaspoon vanilla extract
Dash ground cinnamon
Assorted fresh fruit,
   cut up (optional)

In small bowl, combine all ingredients except fruit. Stir with whisk until smooth. Cover; refrigerate until well chilled. Serve with assorted fresh fruit, if desired. Cover; refrigerate leftover dip.   *10 servings*

```
Nutritional Information Per Serving
         (2 tablespoons dip)
40  Calories              0  mg Cholesterol
 1  gm Protein           20  mg Sodium
 9  gm Carbohydrate      50  mg Calcium
 0  gm Fat
```

PARTY MIX WITH COCOA

½ cup (1 stick) margarine
2 tablespoons sugar
2 tablespoons HERSHEY'S
   Cocoa
3 cups bite-size crisp wheat
   squares cereal

3 cups toasted oat cereal
   rings
2 cups miniature pretzels
1 cup salted peanuts
2 cups raisins

To Microwave: In 4-quart microwave-safe bowl, place margarine. Microwave at HIGH (100%) 1 to 1½ minutes or until melted; stir in sugar and cocoa. Add cereals, pretzels and peanuts to margarine mixture; stir until well coated. Microwave at HIGH 3 minutes, stirring every minute. Stir in raisins. Microwave at HIGH 3 minutes, stirring every minute. Cool completely. Store in airtight container at room temperature.   *10 cups mix*

```
Nutritional Information Per Serving
              (¹/₄ cup)
96  Calories              0  mg Cholesterol
 2  gm Protein          120  mg Sodium
13  gm Carbohydrate      10  mg Calcium
 4  gm Fat
```

HOT COCOA WITH CINNAMON

3 tablespoons sugar
3 tablespoons HERSHEY'S
    Cocoa
½ cup hot water

1 (3-inch) piece stick
    cinnamon
3 cups skim milk
½ teaspoon vanilla extract

In medium saucepan, stir together sugar and cocoa; gradually stir in water. Add cinnamon. Cook over medium heat, stirring constantly, until mixture boils; boil and stir 1 minute. Immediately stir in milk; continue cooking and stirring until mixture is hot. *Do not boil.* Remove from heat; discard cinnamon stick. Stir in vanilla. Beat with rotary beater or whisk until foamy. Serve immediately.

Four 7-ounce servings

Nutritional Information Per Serving	
120 Calories	5 mg Cholesterol
7 gm Protein	95 mg Sodium
20 gm Carbohydrate	240 mg Calcium
1 gm Fat	

CREAMY CHOCOLATE CUPCAKE FROSTING

¼ cup (½ stick) extra light
    corn oil spread, softened
2¾ cups powdered sugar

½ cup HERSHEY'S Cocoa
⅓ cup plain nonfat yogurt
½ teaspoon vanilla extract

In small mixer bowl, beat corn oil spread on medium speed of electric mixer until creamy. Add powdered sugar and cocoa alternately with yogurt; beat to spreading consistency. Blend in vanilla. Use frosting immediately. Cover; refrigerate leftover frosting and frosted cupcakes.

1¾ cups frosting; frosts 24 cupcakes

Nutritional Information Per Serving **(1 tablespoon frosting only)**	
60 Calories	0 mg Cholesterol
1 gm Protein	10 mg Sodium
13 gm Carbohydrate	10 mg Calcium
1 gm Fat	

Hot Cocoa with Cinnamon

CHOCO-LOWFAT MUFFINS

1½ cups all-purpose flour
¾ cup granulated sugar
¼ cup HERSHEY'S Cocoa
    or HERSHEY'S European
    Style Cocoa
2 teaspoons baking powder
1 teaspoon baking soda

½ teaspoon salt
⅔ cup vanilla lowfat yogurt
⅔ cup skim milk
½ teaspoon vanilla extract
    Powdered sugar
    (optional)

Heat oven to 400°F. Line 14 muffin cups (2½ inches in diameter) with paper bake cups. In medium bowl, stir together flour, granulated sugar, cocoa, baking powder, baking soda and salt; stir in yogurt, milk and vanilla just until combined. *(Do not beat.)* Fill muffin cups ⅔ full with batter.

Bake 15 to 20 minutes or until wooden pick inserted in centers comes out clean. Cool slightly in pans on wire racks. Remove from pans. Sprinkle powdered sugar over tops of muffins, if desired. Serve warm. Store, covered, at room temperature or freeze in airtight container for longer storage.   *14 muffins*

Nutritional Information Per Serving	
(1 muffin)	
100 Calories	0 mg Cholesterol
2 gm Protein	200 mg Sodium
22 gm Carbohydrate	45 mg Calcium
1 gm Fat	

CHOCOBERRY REFRESHER

1¼ cups cold lowfat milk
1 container (8 ounces)
        vanilla lowfat yogurt
¼ cup HERSHEY'S Syrup

¼ cup HERSHEY'S Strawberry
    Syrup
    Ice cubes (optional)

In blender container, place all ingredients except ice cubes. Cover; blend until smooth. Pour into 3 glasses over ice cubes, if desired. Serve immediately.   *Three 8-ounce servings*

Nutritional Information Per Serving	
170 Calories	10 mg Cholesterol
8 gm Protein	120 mg Sodium
30 gm Carbohydrate	270 mg Calcium
3 gm Fat	

CHOCOLATE CITRUS SHAKE

1 cup orange juice
½ cup nonfat dry milk powder
½ cup crushed ice
½ of ripe medium banana
⅓ cup plain nonfat yogurt
¼ cup powdered sugar

2 tablespoons HERSHEY'S Cocoa or HERSHEY'S European Style Cocoa
1 teaspoon strawberry extract
Additional crushed ice (optional)

In blender container, place all ingredients except additional crushed ice. Cover; blend until smooth. Pour into 3 glasses over additional crushed ice, if desired. Serve immediately.

Three 8-ounce servings

Nutritional Information Per Serving

160	Calories	0	mg Cholesterol
7	gm Protein	85	mg Sodium
31	gm Carbohydrate	205	mg Calcium
1	gm Fat		

HOT COCOA AU LAIT

2 tablespoons HERSHEY'S Cocoa or HERSHEY'S European Style Cocoa
¼ cup hot water
1½ cups skim milk

Granulated sugar substitute to equal 8 teaspoons sugar
¼ teaspoon vanilla extract

In small saucepan, place cocoa; gradually stir in water. Cook over medium heat, stirring constantly, until mixture boils; boil and stir until smooth and hot, about 1 minute. Immediately stir in milk; continue cooking and stirring until mixture is hot. *Do not boil.* Remove from heat; stir in sugar substitute and vanilla. Serve immediately.

Three 5-ounce servings

Nutritional Information Per Serving

70	Calories	2	mg Cholesterol
5	gm Protein	65	mg Sodium
9	gm Carbohydrate	155	mg Calcium
1	gm Fat		

Index

Bar Cookies
Chocolate Mousse Squares, 36
Choco-Lowfat Strawberry Shortbread
  Bars, 42
Crispy Cocoa Bars, 47
Fudgey Brownie Cut-Outs, 39
Beverages
Chocoberry Refresher, 92
Chocolate Citrus Shake, 93
Hot Cocoa au Lait, 93
Hot Cocoa with Cinnamon, 90
Peachy Chocolate Yogurt Shake, 86
Skim Milk Hot Cocoa, 88
Slimming Chocoberry Splash, 84
Breads
Choco-Lowfat Muffins, 92
Orange Chocolate Chip Bread, 80
Brownies (*see* **Bar Cookies; Cookies**)

Cakes (*see also* **Cheesecakes**)
Chocolate and Raspberry Cream Torte,
  18
Chocolate Cake Fingers, 6
Chocolate Cherry Angel Delight, 30
Chocolate Cinnamon Snacking Cake,
  24
Chocolate Cupcakes, 25
Chocolate Lemon Cake, 11
Chocolate Orange Cake, 11
Chocolate Roulade with Creamy Yogurt
  Filling, 22
Cocoa Apple Snack Cake, 31
Easy Chocolate-Cheese-Filled Angel
  Cake, 20
Elegant Chocolate Angel Torte, 34
Four Way Fudgey Chocolate Cake, 30
Fudgey Chocolate Cupcakes, 32
Hershey's Slimmed Down Chocolate
  Cake, 28
Marbled Angel Cake, 16
Secret Strawberry Filled Angel Cake, 12
Slenderific Brownie Snacking Cakes, 10
Sunburst Chocolate Cake, 14
Swiss Cocoa Squares, 10
Caribbean Freeze, 52
Cheesecakes
Chocolate Swirled Cheesecake, 26
Cocoa Cheesecake with Ricotta
  Cheese, 21
Luscious Chocolate Cheesecake, 8
Trimmed Down Chocoberry
  Cheesecake, 35
Chocoberry Refresher, 92
Chocolate and Raspberry Cream Torte, 18

Chocolate-Banana Sherbet, 72
Chocolate-Banana Yogurt Freeze, 54
Chocolate Cake Fingers, 6
Chocolate Cherry Angel Delight, 30
Chocolate Cinnamon Snacking Cake,
  24
Chocolate Citrus Shake, 93
Chocolate Clouds, 46
Chocolate Cream Pie with Skim Milk, 82
Chocolate Cupcakes, 25
Chocolate Dessert Timbales, 63
Chocolate-Filled Meringue Shells with
  Strawberry Sauce, 60
Chocolate Filling, 60
Chocolate Fruit Dip, 89
Chocolate Glaze, 16, 38
Chocolate Lemon Cake, 11
Chocolate Mint Glaze, 46
Chocolate Mint Meringues, 46
Chocolate Mousse Squares, 36
Chocolate Orange Cake, 11
Chocolate-Orange Ice, 55
Chocolate Orange Meringues, 38
Chocolate Roulade with Creamy Yogurt
  Filling, 22
Chocolate Sauce, 48
Chocolate Sauce and Ice Milk, 88
Chocolate Swirled Cheesecake, 26
Chocolate Syrup Whipped Topping, 12
Chocolate Yogurt Creme Pudding, 76
Choco-Lowfat Muffins, 92
Choco-Lowfat Strawberry Shortbread Bars,
  42
Choco-Orange Fluff, 70
Citrus Filling, 14
Cocoa Apple Snack Cake, 31
Cocoa-Banana Freeze, 62
Cocoa Cheesecake with Ricotta Cheese,
  21
Cocoa Fruit Balls, 82
Cocoa Glaze, 40
Cocoa Pudding, 52
Cookies (*see also* **Bar Cookies**)
Chocolate Clouds, 46
Chocolate Mint Meringues, 46
Chocolate Orange Meringues, 38
Double Chocolate Sugar Cookies, 38
Mini Brownie Cups, 44
Sunny Cocoa Drop Cookies, 40
Creamy Chocolate and Peach Layered
  Pudding, 64
Creamy Chocolate Cupcake Frosting, 90
Creamy Yogurt Filling, 24
Crispy Cocoa Bars, 47

Desserts, Chilled
   Chocolate Dessert Timbales, 63
   Chocolate-Filled Meringue Shells with
     Strawberry Sauce, 60
   Chocolate Yogurt Creme Pudding, 76
   Choco-Orange Fluff, 70
   Cocoa Pudding, 52
   Creamy Chocolate and Peach Layered
     Pudding, 64
   Fruit in a Chocolate Cloud, 56
   Lighter Than Air Chocolate Almond
     Parfaits, 78
   Lighter Than Air Chocolate Delight, 70
   Luscious Cold Chocolate Souffles, 50
   Shamrock Parfaits, 68
   Silky Cocoa Creme, 62
   Slimming Chocolate Mousse, 71
   Tempting Chocolate Mousse, 79
   Tidal Wave Cocoa Almond Mousse, 54
   Waist-Watcher's Cocoa Dessert, 74
Desserts, Frozen
   Caribbean Freeze, 52
   Chocolate-Banana Sherbet, 72
   Chocolate-Banana Yogurt Freeze, 54
   Chocolate-Orange Ice, 55
   Cocoa-Banana Freeze, 62
   Frosty Chocolate and Vanilla Mini
     Bombes, 66
   Fruit-Filled Chocolate Dreams, 48
   Refreshing Cocoa-Fruit Sherbet, 76
   Tropical Chocolate Orange Ice Milk, 58
Double Chocolate Sugar Cookies, 38

Easy Chocolate-Cheese-Filled Angel
   Cake, 20
Elegant Chocolate Angel Torte, 34

Fillings
   Chocolate Filling, 60
   Citrus Filling, 14
   Creamy Yogurt Filling, 24
   Raspberry Cream, 18
Four Way Fudgey Chocolate Cake, 30
Frostings & Glazes
   Chocolate Glaze, 16, 38
   Chocolate Mint Glaze, 46
   Cocoa Glaze, 40
   Creamy Chocolate Cupcake Frosting, 90
   Light Cocoa Frosting, 66
   Mocha Glaze, 44
   Powdered Sugar Glaze, 25
   Slimmed Down Cocoa Almond Frosting,
     28
   Slimmed Down Cocoa Frosting, 28
   Vanilla Chip Drizzle, 42
Frosty Chocolate and Vanilla Mini
   Bombes, 66
Fruit-Filled Chocolate Dreams, 48
Fruit in a Chocolate Cloud, 56
Fudgey Brownie Cut-Outs, 39
Fudgey Chocolate Cupcakes, 32

Graham Crust, 35

Hershey's Basic Cocoa Baking Mix, 84
Hershey's Slimmed Down Chocolate
   Cake, 28

Hot Cocoa au Lait, 93
Hot Cocoa with Cinnamon, 90

Light Cocoa Frosting, 66
Lighter Than Air Chocolate Almond
   Parfaits, 78
Lighter Than Air Chocolate Delight, 70
Luscious Chocolate Cheesecake, 8
Luscious Cold Chocolate Souffles, 50

Marbled Angel Cake, 16
Mini Brownie Cups, 44
Mocha Glaze, 44

Orange Chocolate Chip Bread, 80
Orange Cups, 58

Party Mix with Cocoa, 89
Peach Sauce, 24, 64
Peachy Chocolate Yogurt Shake, 86
Peanut Butter 'n' Chocolate Chips Snack
   Mix, 83
Pie: Chocolate Cream Pie with Skim Milk,
   82
Powdered Sugar Glaze, 25

Refreshing Cocoa-Fruit Sherbet, 76

Sauces
   Chocolate Sauce, 48
   Chocolate Sauce and Ice Milk, 88
   Peach Sauce, 24, 64
   Sinfully Rich Nonfat Fudge Sauce, 86
Secret Strawberry Filled Angel Cake, 12
Shamrock Parfaits, 68
Silky Cocoa Creme, 62
Sinfully Rich Nonfat Fudge Sauce, 86
Skim Milk Hot Cocoa, 88
Slenderific Brownie Snacking Cakes, 10
Slimmed Down Cocoa Almond Frosting,
   28
Slimmed Down Cocoa Frosting, 28
Slimming Chocoberry Splash, 84
Slimming Chocolate Mousse, 71
Snacks
   Chocolate Fruit Dip, 89
   Cocoa Fruit Balls, 82
   Party Mix with Cocoa, 89
   Peanut Butter 'n' Chocolate Chips
     Snack Mix, 83
Sunburst Chocolate Cake, 14
Sunny Cocoa Drop Cookies, 40
Swiss Cocoa Squares, 10

Tempting Chocolate Mousse, 79
Tidal Wave Cocoa Almond Mousse, 54
Trimmed Down Chocoberry Cheesecake,
   35
Tropical Chocolate Orange Ice Milk, 58

Vanilla Chip Drizzle, 42
Vanilla Wafer Crust, 21

Waist-Watcher's Cocoa Dessert, 74

Yogurt Cheese, 20, 24, 26, 56
Yogurt Topping, 8

METRIC CONVERSION CHART

VOLUME MEASUREMENTS (dry)

$^1/_8$ teaspoon = 0.5 mL
$^1/_4$ teaspoon = 1 mL
$^1/_2$ teaspoon = 2 mL
$^3/_4$ teaspoon = 4 mL
1 teaspoon = 5 mL
1 tablespoon = 15 mL
2 tablespoons = 30 mL
$^1/_4$ cup = 60 mL
$^1/_3$ cup = 75 mL
$^1/_2$ cup = 125 mL
$^2/_3$ cup = 150 mL
$^3/_4$ cup = 175 mL
1 cup = 250 mL
2 cups = 1 pint = 500 mL
3 cups = 750 mL
4 cups = 1 quart = 1 L

VOLUME MEASUREMENTS (fluid)

1 fluid ounce (2 tablespoons) = 30 mL
4 fluid ounces ($^1/_2$ cup) = 125 mL
8 fluid ounces (1 cup) = 250 mL
12 fluid ounces (1$^1/_2$ cups) = 375 mL
16 fluid ounces (2 cups) = 500 mL

WEIGHTS (mass)

$^1/_2$ ounce = 15 g
1 ounce = 30 g
3 ounces = 90 g
4 ounces = 120 g
8 ounces = 225 g
10 ounces = 285 g
12 ounces = 360 g
16 ounces = 1 pound = 450 g

DIMENSIONS

$^1/_{16}$ inch = 2 mm
$^1/_8$ inch = 3 mm
$^1/_4$ inch = 6 mm
$^1/_2$ inch = 1.5 cm
$^3/_4$ inch = 2 cm
1 inch = 2.5 cm

OVEN TEMPERATURES

250°F = 120°C
275°F = 140°C
300°F = 150°C
325°F = 160°C
350°F = 180°C
375°F = 190°C
400°F = 200°C
425°F = 220°C
450°F = 230°C

BAKING PAN SIZES

Utensil	Size in Inches/Quarts	Metric Volume	Size in Centimeters
Baking or Cake Pan (square or rectangular)	8×8×2	2 L	20×20×5
	9×9×2	2.5 L	22×22×5
	12×8×2	3 L	30×20×5
	13×9×2	3.5 L	33×23×5
Loaf Pan	8×4×3	1.5 L	20×10×7
	9×5×3	2 L	23×13×7
Round Layer Cake Pan	8×1½	1.2 L	20×4
	9×1½	1.5 L	23×4
Pie Plate	8×1¼	750 mL	20×3
	9×1¼	1 L	23×3
Baking Dish or Casserole	1 quart	1 L	—
	1½ quart	1.5 L	—
	2 quart	2 L	—